# At Box of Crayons we give busy managers practical tools so they can coach in 10 minutes or less.

Coaching is a foundational skill for every manager and leader. When people make coaching an everyday way of working, they create more focus, more courage and more resilience. They help others (and themselves) work less hard and have more impact. **You can learn about Box of Crayons' coaching programs at BoxOfCrayons.biz**

Want to buy a lot of these? Fantastic. We can help. We can also customize and co-brand *The Coaching Habit*. Please contact us at orders@boxofcrayons.biz for more information.

## Praise for **The Coaching Habit**

Michael Bungay Stanier distills the essentials of coaching to seven core questions. And if you master his simple yet profound technique, you'll get a two-fer. You'll provide more effective support to your employees and co-workers. And you may find that you become the ultimate coach for yourself.

**DANIEL H. PINK**, author of **To Sell Is Human** and **Drive**

Coaching is an art, and it's far easier said than done. It takes courage to ask a question rather than offer up advice, provide an answer or unleash a solution. Giving another person the opportunity to find their own way, make their own mistakes and create their own wisdom is both brave and vulnerable. It can also mean unlearning our "fix it" habits. In this practical and inspiring book, Michael shares seven transformative questions that can make a difference in how we lead and support. And he guides us through the tricky part: how to take this new information and turn it into habits and a daily practice.

**BRENÉ BROWN**, author of **Rising Strong** and **Daring Greatly**

What can you do to become a better leader? Michael asks and answers this question by offering aspiring leaders seven thoughtful questions that will change their leadership habits. This book is full of practical, useful and interesting questions, ideas and tools that will guide any leader trying to be better.

**DAVE ULRICH**, co-author of **The Why of Work** and **The Leadership Code**

Michael's intelligence, wit, articulateness and dedication to the craft of coaching shine forth in this brilliant how-to manual for anyone called to assist others. Even after four decades of my own experience in this arena, *The Coaching Habit* has provided me with great takeaways.

**DAVID ALLEN**, author of **Getting Things Done**

Amid a sea of coaching books that drone on with the same old, over-used conceptual frameworks, there is a gem of hope. *The Coaching Habit* is a treasure trove of practical wisdom that takes a timeless pursuit—to turn every manager into a coach—and breaks it down into a simple set of everyday habits. If you are ready to take your leadership to the next level, you need this book.

**JESSICA AMORTEGUI**, Senior Director Learning & Development, Logitech

There are many coaching books out there that end up on the bookshelf half read. Michael Bungay Stanier's *The Coaching Habit* engages you from start to finish. A simple read that is bold and direct, relatable and real, this book will change the way you communicate with colleagues at work and family at home. If you want to read one book on coaching that will resonate with you quickly and that is not overwhelming, choose this one.

**JOHANNE McNALLY MYERS**, VP Human Resources, Tim Hortons

Among a plethora of books, studies and op-ed pieces about the importance of coaching and how to execute this most critical of development interventions well, it's easy to understand why students and practitioners of the craft feel confused or overwhelmed by the array of approaches, frameworks and systems extolled as "the right way." Michael Bungay Stanier has expertly cut through this confusion with his new book in a manner that is simple to understand, realistic in its intention and ultimately effective to apply. I believe this book will establish itself as a powerful and useful toolset for the professional coach, the student learner and the people manager alike.

**STUART CRABB**, Director Learning & Development, Facebook

This is not just a book; this is the voice in your head, the person that sits on your shoulder—guiding you to greatness. Being a great coach is more than skill; it's a mindset, a way of being. Michael has a remarkable way of delivering that message through artful storytelling, practical examples and proven techniques. A must-have book for the coach who truly wants to make a difference.

**SINÉAD CONDON**, Head of Global
Performance Enablement, CA Technologies

*The Coaching Habit* is funny, smart, practical, memorable and grounded in current behavioural science. I found it highly valuable for my own work and collaborations.

**JAMES SLEZAK**, Executive Director of Strategy, **New York Times**

Where others can overcomplicate the purpose and practice of coaching, Michael Bungay Stanier provides a practical and unintimidating approach to this essential habit of great leaders. He succinctly articulates the research behind the art of respectful inquiry and its role in fostering an authentic partnership among colleagues who are committed to doing meaningful work together. *The Coaching Habit* is a thoroughly enjoyable read that immediately inspired me to adopt new habits.

· **DANA WOODS**, CEO, American Association of Critical-Care Nurses

The magic of leadership occurs in daily conversations. With *The Coaching Habit,* Michael Bungay Stanier gives managers an extremely simple yet powerful tool (just seven questions!) to help them coach their teams to greatness, each and every day.

**ANDREW COLLIER**, Head of Leadership Development, Nestlé

"*Fantastic . . .* and *Where was this book when I needed it?*" are the first thoughts popping into my head after reading this book. I've read countless books on leadership and coaching over my career but few brought it all together like Michael Bungay Stanier's. I love the concepts of keeping it simple and practice, practice, practice, which are key to building your coaching habit. Michael makes what some leaders see as complex a simple process, whether you are an experienced or new people leader. Definitely a must-read book.

**MONIQUE BATEMAN**, SVP, TD Bank Group

*The Coaching Habit* is the essence of practical coaching for busy managers. No filler, no abstract theory, no tedious stories. Just everyday, practical tools so that you can coach in ten minutes or less.

**MELISSA DAIMLER**, Head of Learning &
Organizational Development, Twitter

Bungay Stanier has it right. We are creatures of habit, and from our habits we create ourselves, our lives and the world around us. *The Coaching Habit* is a manual for applying the power of habit to the power of coaching to accomplish more with and through others. Do not read this book. Practice it. Apply it. Keep it on your desk and build your coaching habit.

**MICHELE MILAN**, CEO Executive Programs,
Rotman School of Management, University of Toronto

# The Coaching Habit Say Less, Ask More & Change the Way You Lead Forever

# Say Less, Ask More & Change the Way You Lead Forever

Michael
Bungay
Stanier

# The Coaching Habit

BOX OF CRAYONS PRESS

# TO **MARCELLA**

Want to buy a lot of these? Fantastic. We can help. We can
also customize and co-brand *The Coaching Habit*. Please
contact us at orders@boxofcrayons.biz for more information.

Box of Crayons Press
137 Marion Street
Toronto ON Canada  M6R 1E6
www.boxofcrayons.biz

Catalogue data available from Library and Archives Canada
ISBN 978-0-9784407-4-9 (Paperback)
ISBN 978-0-9784407-5-6 (Ebook)

Cover and text design by Peter Cocking
Printed and bound in Canada by Marquis

16  17  18  19  20    5  4  3  2  1

**Harlan Howard said every great country song has three chords and the truth.**

This book gives you seven questions and the tools to make them an everyday way to work less hard and have more impact.

# Contents

**You Need a Coaching Habit**   *1*

**How to Build a Habit**   *15*

**Question Masterclass Part 1:**
Ask One Question at a Time   *29*

1 **The Kickstart Question**   *35*

**Question Masterclass Part 2:**
Cut the Intro and Ask the Question   *49*

2 **The AWE Question**   *55*

**Question Masterclass Part 3:**
Should You Ask Rhetorical Questions?   *73*

3 **The Focus Question**   *79*

**Question Masterclass Part 4:**
Stick to Questions Starting with "What"   *99*

**An Irresistible 1-2-3 Combination**   *105*

**4 The Foundation Question**   *109*

**Question Masterclass Part 5:**
Get Comfortable with Silence   *127*

**5 The Lazy Question**   *133*

**Question Masterclass Part 6:**
Actually Listen to the Answer   *153*

**6 The Strategic Question**   *159*

**Question Masterclass Part 7:**
Acknowledge the Answers You Get   *179*

**7 The Learning Question**   *185*

**Question Masterclass Part 8:**
Use Every Channel to Ask a Question   *201*

**Conclusion**   *207*

A Treasure Trove of Additional Awesomeness   *215*

Acknowledgments   *225*

# You Need a Coaching Habit

Everyone now knows that managers and leaders **need to coach their people.**

The leadership press has endless articles about it. Assorted gurus suggest that coaching is an essential leadership behaviour. The number of executive coaches seems to be multiplying according to Moore's Law. Even Dilbert mocks coaching—and there's no surer sign of mainstream success than that.

Daniel Goleman, the psychologist and journalist who popularized the concept of emotional intelligence, put a stake in the ground more than fifteen years ago in his *Harvard Business Review* article "Leadership That Gets Results." He suggested that there are six essential leadership styles. Coaching was one of them and it was shown to have a "markedly positive" impact on performance, climate (culture) and the bottom line. At the same time, it was the least-used leadership style. Why? Goleman wrote, "Many leaders told us they don't have the time in this high-pressure economy for the slow and tedious work of teaching people and helping them grow."

And remember, this was in the halcyon days of 2000, when email was still a blessing, not a curse, globalization was just warming up, and we hadn't yet sold our souls to our smartphones. My experience these days, working with busy managers around the world, tells me that things have, if anything, got worse rather than better. We're all stretched more thinly than ever. And while "coaching" is now a more commonly used term, the actual practice of coaching still doesn't seem to be occurring that often. And when it does, it doesn't seem to work.

## You've Probably Already Tried. And Failed.

The odds are you've already come across coaching in some form. Research in 2006 from leadership development firm BlessingWhite suggested that 73 percent of managers had some form of coaching training. So far so good. However, it seems it wasn't very *good* coaching training. Only 23 percent of people being coached—yes, fewer than one in four—thought that the coaching had a significant impact on their performance or job satisfaction. Ten percent even suggested that the coaching they were getting was having a negative effect. (Can you imagine what it would be like going into those meetings? "I look forward to being more confused and less motivated after my coaching session with you.")

You're probably **not getting** very effective coaching, and you're probably **not delivering** very effective coaching.

So, in summary: You're probably not getting very effective coaching; and you're probably not delivering very effective coaching.

My guess is that there are at least three reasons why your first go at developing a coaching habit didn't stick. The first reason is that the coaching training you got was probably overly theoretical, too complicated, a little boring and divorced from the reality of your busy work life. One of those training sessions, perhaps, where you caught up on your email backlog.

Even if the training was engaging—here's reason number two—you likely didn't spend much time figuring out how to translate the new insights into action so you'd do things differently. When you got back to the office, the status quo flexed its impressive muscles, got you in a headlock and soon had you doing things exactly the way you'd done them before.

The third reason is that the seemingly simple behaviour change of giving a little less advice and asking a few more questions is surprisingly difficult. You've spent years delivering advice and getting promoted and praised for it. You're seen to be "adding value" and you've the added bonus of staying in control of the situation. On the other hand, when you're asking questions, you might feel less certain about whether you're being useful, the conversation can feel slower and you might feel like you've somewhat lost control of the conversation (and indeed you have. That's called "empowering"). Put like that, it doesn't sound like that good an offer.

## But It's Not That Hard. Really.

At my company, Box of Crayons, we've trained more than ten thousand busy managers like you in practical coaching skills. Over the years, we've come to hold these truths to be self-evident:

- Coaching is simple. In fact, this book's *Seven Essential Questions* give you most of what you need.

- You can coach someone in *ten minutes or less*. And in today's busy world, you have to be able to coach in ten minutes or less.

- Coaching should be *a daily, informal act*, not an occasional, formal "It's Coaching Time!" event.

- You can *build a coaching habit*, but only if you understand and use the proven mechanics of building and embedding new habits.

But why bother to change things up? Why would you want to build a coaching habit?

## Here's Why It's Worth the Effort

The essence of coaching lies in helping others and unlocking their potential. But I'm sure you're already committed to being helpful, and that hasn't led to your coaching more often.

You're already committed to being helpful, **and that hasn't led to your coaching more often.**

So let's look at why coaching others helps *you*. It lets you work less hard and have more impact. When you build a coaching habit, you can more easily break out of three vicious circles that plague our workplaces: creating overdependence, getting overwhelmed and becoming disconnected.

## Circle #1: Creating Overdependence

You may find that you've become part of an *overdependent* team. There's a double whammy here. First, you've trained your people to become excessively reliant on you, a situation that turns out to be disempowering for them and frustrating for you. And then as an unwelcome bonus, because you've been so successful in creating this dependency that you now have too much work to do, you may also have become a bottleneck in the system. Everyone loses momentum and motivation. The more you help your people, the more they seem to need your help. The more they need your help, the more time you spend helping them.

Building a coaching habit will help your team be more self-sufficient by increasing their autonomy and sense of mastery and by reducing your need to jump in, take over and become the bottleneck.

## Circle #2: Getting Overwhelmed

You may also be *overwhelmed* by the quantity of work you have. It doesn't matter if you've mastered all the productivity hacks in the world; the faster you dig, the faster the world keeps flooding in. As you're pulled in different directions by proliferating priorities, distracted by the relentless ping of email and hustling from meeting to meeting, you lose focus. The more you lose focus, the more overwhelmed you feel. The more overwhelmed you feel, the more you lose focus.

Building a coaching habit will help you regain focus so you and your team can do the work that has real impact and so you can direct your time, energy and resources to solving the challenges that make a difference.

### Circle #3: Becoming Disconnected

Finally, you may be *disconnected* from the work that matters. My previous book *Do More Great Work* had as its foundation the principle that it's not enough just to get things done. You have to help people do more of the work that has impact *and* meaning. The more we do work that has no real purpose, the less engaged and motivated we are. The less engaged we are, the less likely we are to find and create Great Work.

Building a coaching habit will help you and your team reconnect to the work that not only has impact but has meaning as well. Coaching can fuel the courage to step out beyond the comfortable and familiar, can help people learn from their experiences and can literally and metaphorically increase and help fulfil a person's potential.

WHAT PEOPLE
THINK OF AS THE
MOMENT OF DIS-
COVERY IS REALLY
**THE DISCOVERY
OF THE QUESTION.**

Jonas Salk

So you're up against the Bind, the Grind and the Resigned. And building a coaching habit is a way of breaking through to a better way of working.

## The Seven Essential Questions

At the heart of the book are seven questions that will break you out of these three vicious circles and elevate the way you work. The questions work not only with your direct reports but also with customers, suppliers, colleagues, bosses and even (occasionally and, obviously, with no guarantees offered) spouses and teenage children. These questions have the potential to transform your weekly check-in one-to-ones, your team meetings, your sales meetings and (particularly important) those non-meeting moments when you just bump into someone between scheduled events.

The *Kickstart Question* is the way to start any conversation in a way that's both focused and open. The *AWE Question*—the best coaching question in the world—works as a self-management tool for you, and as a boost for the other six questions here. The *Focus Question* and the *Foundation Question* are about getting to the heart of the challenge, so you've got your attention on what really matters. The *Lazy Question* will save you hours, while the *Strategic Question* will save hours for those you're working with. And the *Learning Question*, which pairs with the *Kickstart Question* to make the Coaching Bookends, will ensure that everyone finds their interactions with you more useful.

## Shall We Begin?

Are you ready to go? I'm sure you're keen to get to the Seven Essential Questions, but before we go there, we're going to take a short detour into the nitty-gritty of how to change your behaviour. There's no point in giving you useful tools unless you can put them into action. The next chapter, on the New Habit Formula, helps with that. In it you'll learn why the starting place for a new habit isn't the new behaviour after all, why sixty seconds matter so much and how the New Habit Formula can be your engine for focused behaviour change.

# How to Build a Habit

**In which we unpack the real science of how to change your behaviour**, rather than relying on the myths and lies that you'll find on the Internet.

The change of behaviour at the heart of what this book is about is this: a little more asking people questions and a little less telling people what to do. But simple doesn't mean easy, and theory's no good if you don't know how to put it into practice. So before we look at *what* to change, we need to understand *how* to change.

You already know it's hard to change old ways of behaving, however good your intentions. Or is it just me who has:

- sworn not to check email first thing in the morning, and nonetheless found myself in the wee small hours, my face lit by that pale screen glow;

- intended to find inner peace through the discipline of meditation, yet couldn't find five minutes to just sit and breathe, sit and breathe;

- committed to take a proper lunch break, and somehow found myself shaking the crumbs out of my keyboard, evidence of sandwich spillage; or decided to abstain from drinking for a while, and yet had a glass of good Australian shiraz mysteriously appear in my hand at the end of the day?

All that's less surprising when you realize that a Duke University study says that at least 45 percent of our waking behaviour is habitual. Although we'd like to think we're in charge, it turns out that we're not so much controlling how we act with our conscious mind as we are being driven by our subconscious or unconscious mind. It's amazing; also, it's a little disturbing.

There's always been a lot of information out there on how to change the way you behave. Or more accurately, there's a dense jungle of misinformation that grows particularly lush at the turn of each year, when resolutions are in the air. Have you heard the one that says that if you do something for twenty-one days, you'll have a new habit? Someone just made that up, and it now stalks the Internet like a zombie, refusing to die.

Happily, there has been an increase of grounded findings, based on neuroscience and behavioural economics, that have helped clear a path over the last few years. To build an effective new habit, you need five essential components: a reason, a trigger, a micro-habit, effective practice, and a plan.

### Make a Vow

Why would you bother doing something as difficult as changing the way you work? You need to get clear on the payoff for changing something as familiar and efficient (not the same, of course, as effective) as an old behaviour. Getting clear *doesn't* mean imagining success, funnily enough. Research shows that if you spend too much time imagining the outcome, you're less motivated to actually do the work to get there. Leo Babauta frames a helpful way of connecting to the big picture in his book *Zen Habits: Mastering the Art of Change*. He talks about making a vow that's connected to serving others. Leo gave up smoking as a commitment to his wife and newborn daughter. So think less about what your habit can do for you, and more about how this new habit will help a person or people you care about.

### Figure Your Trigger

One key insight from reading Charles Duhigg's book, *The Power of Habit*, is this: if you don't know what triggers the old behaviour, you'll never change it because you'll already be doing it before you know it. The more specific you can be when defining your trigger moment, the more useful a piece of data it is. As an example, "At the team meeting" becomes more usable when it's "When I'm asked to check in at the team meeting" and becomes even more usable when it's "When Jenny asks me for feedback on her idea in the team meeting." With that degree of specificity, you have the starting point for building a strong new habit.

## Double-S It: Be Short & Specific

If you define your new habit in an abstract and slightly vague way, you won't get traction. If it takes too long to do, your big brain will find a way to hack your good intentions. B.J. Fogg's work at tinyhabits.com suggests that you should define your new habit as a micro-habit that needs to take less than sixty seconds to complete. It's about getting really clear on the first step or two that might lead to the bigger habit. The Double-S guideline works particularly well for this book, as each one of the Seven Essential Questions fits that bill.

## Practice Deeply

For his book *The Talent Code*, Dan Coyle researched why certain parts of the world were talent "hot spots" for certain skills. Brazil: soccer. Moscow: women's tennis. New York: music (think the Julliard School). One key factor in each hot spot was knowing how to practice well—Coyle calls it "Deep Practice." The three components of Deep Practice are:

- Practicing small chunks of the bigger action (for instance, rather than practice the whole tennis serve, you practice just tossing the ball up).

- Repetition, repetition and repetition... and repetition. Do it fast, do it slow, do it differently. But keep repeating the action.

PLEASE GIVE
ME SOME GOOD
ADVICE IN YOUR
NEXT LETTER.
**I PROMISE NOT
TO FOLLOW IT.**

Edna St. Vincent Millay

- And finally, being mindful and noticing when it goes well. When it does, celebrate success. You don't have to go buy the bottle of Möet, although you can if you wish. A small fist pump will do just fine.

### Plan How to Get Back on Track

When you stumble—and everyone stumbles—it's easy to give up. "I may as well eat the rest of the cake, seeing as I've now had a slice." In his book *Making Habits, Breaking Habits,* Jeremy Dean helps us face the reality that we will not achieve perfection in our quest to build the habit. We will miss a moment, miss a day. That's a given. What you need to know is what to do when that happens. Resilient systems build in fail-safes so that when something breaks down, the next step to recover is obvious. Make your habit a resilient system.

## Put It All Together: The New Habit Formula

In the Box of Crayons' coaching skills workshops, we've increasingly focused on helping participants define and commit to specific habits (rather than to the broad and rarely acted upon action list). To help people do that, we've drawn from some of the insights above and, after testing it out in the real world, created the New Habit Formula: a simple, straightforward and effective way of articulating and kickstarting the new behaviour you want.

There are three parts to the formula: identifying the trigger, identifying the old habit and defining the new behaviour. Here's how it works.

### Identifying the Trigger: When This Happens…

Define the trigger, the moment when you're at a crossroads and could go down either the well-trod road of the old way of behaving or the Robert Frost path less trodden. If you don't know what this moment is, you're going to continually miss it and, with that, the opportunity to change your behaviour.

Hear an interview with **CHARLES DUHIGG** at the Great Work Podcast.

The more specific you can make it, the better. Charles Duhigg says that there are just five types of triggers: location, time, emotional state, other people, and the immediately preceding action. You can see how you might use a number of them to define a very specific trigger. For instance, a trigger might be "When I'm feeling frustrated (emotional state) in my weekly meeting (time) with Bob (people) because he says 'I haven't really thought about it (action).'"

### Identifying the Old Habit: Instead Of…

Articulate the old habit, so you know what you're trying to stop doing. Again, the more specific you can make it, the more useful it's going to be. For instance (and to carry on the example above), "I ask Bob, 'Have you thought about X?' and hope he'll get the suggestion that I've disguised as a pseudo-question, all the while thinking bad thoughts about Bob."

### Defining the New Behaviour: I Will...

Define the new behaviour, one that will take sixty seconds or less to do. We know that the fundamental shift of behaviour you're looking to accomplish through this book is to give less advice and show more curiosity. And what's great about the Seven Essential Questions that you're about to discover is that you can definitely ask each one in sixty seconds or less.

So to finish our example, "I will ask Bob, 'So what ideas do you have now?'"

At the end of each chapter on one of the Seven Essential Questions, I'm going to ask you to build your own habit based on that question. We'll keep revisiting these concepts and give you some real examples for each question so you can see how the New Habit Formula and the question work in reality.

**MORE** If you want to dive deeper into the latest findings about building better habits, download a short ebook, *The 7½ Coaching Gurus*, at **www.TheCoachingHabit.com/CoachingGurus**. I get into some real detail about the latest research from authors such as **Charles Duhigg**, **B.J. Fogg**, **Gretchen Rubin**, **Dan Coyle**, **Leo Babauta**, **Nir Eyal**, **Jeremy Dean** and a mysterious "half a guru."

## A Final Word on Building Your Coaching Habit

This stuff is simple, but it's not easy. It's hard to change your behaviour, and it takes courage to have a go at doing something differently, and resilience to keep at it when it doesn't work perfectly the first time (which it won't). It's one of the laws of change that as soon as you try something new, you'll get resistance from somewhere, asking you, in *Diff'rent Strokes* style, "What'chu talkin' about, Willis?" To counter that resistance, follow these tips:

- **Start somewhere easy.** If you're going to manage someone differently, pick someone who might be up for it and is willing to cut you some slack. Or pick someone with whom it's all going so badly that you've got nothing left to lose.

- **Start small.** Don't try to incorporate all the ideas in the book all at once. Start somewhere, and try to master one thing and get it "in your bones." And after that, move on to something else.

- **Buddy up.** Here are the support systems I've got around me to change and embed good behaviour: a coach; a mastermind group, which has weekly check-ins and bi-weekly phone calls; another mastermind group, which checks in every three months; and three habit apps on my iPhone. And I already know this stuff. Get a friend or colleague involved and be each other's check-in, encouragement, practice, cheerleader buddy.

# One of the laws of change: As soon as you try something new, you'll get resistance.

· · · · · · · · · · · · · · · · · · · · · · · ·

• **Get back on the horse.** The habit will slip. It won't always work. You'll feel awkward as you sit in the place of learning known as "conscious incompetence" (an accurate if slightly insulting phrase). It's through deliberate and regular practice that you'll move to "conscious competence," which is a much more pleasant place to be.

## Heed the Philosopher

. . . . . . . . . . . . . . . . . . . . . . . . .

Ovid said, "Nothing is stronger than habit." That's bad news and good news. It's bad news in that your life can easily be a mass of less-than-ideal responses and reactions that you've grooved into your brain. And it's good news because now that you understand the mechanics of habits, you can build your own structures for success. Winston Churchill said that "we shape our buildings; and thereafter they shape us." We live within our habits. So shape the way you want to lead, and build the right coaching habits.

And these new habits can start with the very first thing you ask someone—which is exactly what the next chapter is about.

**WATCH IT WORK**

Watch the short videos at **TheCoachingHabit.com/videos** to deepen your learning and help turn insight into action.

**HOW TO BUILD ROCK-SOLID HABITS**  A fun series of videos featuring zombies, monkeys and an egg, all in the service of explaining how to build a rock-solid habit.

# Question
# Masterclass
# Part 1

# Ask **One** Question at a Time

· · · · · · · · · · · · · · · · · · · · · · · · · ·

**Question Masterclass** lessons
appear throughout the book.
Keep an eye out for them,
and apply them to ensure that
you use the **Seven Essential
Questions** to their full effect.

· · · · · · · · · · · · · · · · · · · · · · · · · ·

**M**y friend Matt May, author of *In Pursuit of Elegance* and *The Laws of Subtraction*, tells the story of the time he first drove through the centre of Paris. Swept into the traffic circle around the landmark Arc de Triomphe, he noticed, quickly, that this was not your typical rotary.

With twelve streets feeding into the roundabout, the normal rules were reversed. Here, the incoming traffic had right of way, while the traffic already in the circle had to wait its turn. Even though the system works—those crazy French!—Matt's experience was one of white-knuckled panic as cars seemed to come at him from all sides.

Hear an interview with **MATT MAY** at the Great Work Podcast.

Sometimes being on the receiving end of someone with a pocketful of questions can be like a moment of Parisian driving. Questions come hurling at you left and right, there's no time to answer any of them and you're left feeling dazed and confused.

Some call it drive-by questioning. And rather than feeling like a supportive conversation, it has the unpleasant vibe of an interrogation.

# Ask one question at a time. Just **one question** at a time.

## Here's Your New Habit

. . . . . . . . . . . . . . . . . . . . . .

WHEN THIS HAPPENS...

After I've asked a question . . .

INSTEAD OF...

Adding another question. And then maybe another question, and then another, because after all, they're all good questions and I'm really curious as to what their answers are . . .

I WILL...

Ask just one question. (And then be quiet while I wait for the answer.)

**WATCH IT WORK**

Watch the short videos at **TheCoachingHabit.com/videos** to deepen your learning and help turn insight into action.

**HOW TO ASK A GREAT QUESTION** Using a funky webinar style, Michael shares the five disciplines required to ask a great question.

**1 The Kickstart Question**

2 The AWE Question

3 The Focus Question

4 The Foundation Question

5 The Lazy Question

6 The Strategic Question

7 The Learning Question

# 1: The Kickstart Question

**In which you discover the power of an opening question** that gets the conversation happening fast and deep.

## Breaking the Ice

A good opening line can make all the difference. "It was the best of times, it was the worst of times…" "A long time ago in a galaxy far, far away…" "Did it hurt when you fell from heaven?"

One of the reasons managers don't coach more often than they do is that they don't know how to start. There's that nagging sense that if you could just get going, you'd be fine. But how do you get going? And if you've ever felt stuck in a conversation that seemed a little superficial or boring or simply not that useful, then one of these three situations might be at play: the Small Talk Tango, the Ossified Agenda, or the Default Diagnosis.

## The Small Talk Tango

Make no mistake, there's a place for small talk. It's a way of reconnecting and engaging with a person, of building relationships, of remembering that other people are human and reminding them that you're human, too. And yet you've felt that sinking feeling when you realize that you've used up eight of your fifteen allotted minutes talking trivia. Those moments when you think, *Seriously, do we always need to discuss that, say, it's cold and snowing in Canada during the winter? Or that sports team, will they ever get any better?* Small talk might be a useful way to warm up, but it's rarely the bridge that leads to a conversation that matters.

## The Ossified Agenda

This situation is commonly found in standing meetings—same time, same people, same place, same agenda. It becomes a dreary recitation of facts and figures, a report that sheds little light and seems to drain energy from the room. The agenda might have been perfect a week, a month or a year ago, but now it's putting process in front of what really matters.

## The Default Diagnosis

There's no question or conversation about what the issue is. You're sure you know what it is. Or they're sure they know what it is. Or maybe you both think you know what it is. And so... *bang!* You're off to the races, pursuing something that, if you're lucky, is approximately-ish the real topic. This response is comfortable and feels like progress because you're solving something. But you're in the wrong hole. Digging faster or smarter isn't going to help.

# The Kickstart Question:
# "What's on Your Mind?"

An almost fail-safe way to start a chat that quickly turns into a real conversation is the question, "What's on your mind?" It's something of a Goldilocks question, walking a fine line so it is neither too open and broad nor too narrow and confining.

Because it's open, it invites people to get to the heart of the matter and share what's most important to them. You're not telling them or guiding them. You're showing them the trust and granting them the autonomy to make the choice for themselves.

And yet the question is focused, too. It's not an invitation to tell you anything or everything. It's encouragement to go right away to what's exciting, what's provoking anxiety, what's all-consuming, what's waking them up at 4 a.m., what's got their hearts beating fast.

It's a question that says, *Let's talk about the thing that matters most*. It's a question that dissolves ossified agendas, sidesteps small talk and defeats the default diagnosis.

And once you've asked it, you can use a framework I call the 3P model to focus the conversation even further. But before we go on to the 3P model, it's useful to understand the difference between two types of coaching.

## Coaching for Performance
## vs. Coaching for Development

Some institutions distinguish between coaching for performance and coaching for development. *Coaching for performance* is about addressing and fixing a specific problem or challenge. It's putting out the fire or building up the fire or banking the fire. It's everyday stuff, and it's important and necessary. *Coaching for development* is about turning the focus from the issue to the person dealing with the issue, the person who's managing the fire. This conversation is more rare and significantly more powerful. If I ask you to think back to a time when someone coached you in a way that stuck and made a difference, I'll bet that it was a coaching-for-development conversation. The focus was on calling you forward to learn, improve and grow, rather than on just getting something sorted out.

The 3P model is a straightforward way to create focus, make the conversation more robust and (when appropriate) shift the focus to the more powerful level that's coaching for development.

## Deepen Focus with the 3Ps

The 3P model is a framework for choosing what to focus on in a coaching conversation—for deciding which aspect of a challenge might be at the heart of a difficulty that the person is

**Call them forward to learn, improve and grow**, rather than to just get something sorted out.

ANSWERS ARE **CLOSED ROOMS**; AND QUESTIONS ARE **OPEN DOORS** THAT INVITE US IN.

Nancy Willard

working through. A challenge might typically be centred on a project, a person or a pattern of behaviour.

## Projects

A project is the content of the situation, the stuff that's being worked on. It's the easiest place to go to and it will be the most familiar to most of us. We spend our days finding solutions to challenges, and our eyes are almost always on the situation at hand. This realm is where coaching for performance and technical change tends to occur. Often, the art is in knowing how to start here and then seeing whether the conversation would benefit from including one or both of the other two Ps.

## People

Have you ever thought, *Work would be easy if it weren't for all these annoying people*? Surely it's not just me. Certainly, situations are always made more complex when you—in all your imperfect, not-always-rational, messy, biased, hasn't-fully-obtained-enlightenment glory—have to work with others who, surprisingly, are also imperfect, not always rational, messy, biased, and a few steps short of full wisdom and compassion.

When you're talking about people, though, you're not really talking about them. You're talking about a relationship and, specifically, about what your role is in this relationship that might currently be less than ideal.

## Patterns

Here you're looking at patterns of behaviour and ways of work-ing that you'd like to change. This area is most likely where coaching-for-development conversations will emerge. They are personal and challenging, and they provide a place where people's self-knowledge and potential can grow and flourish. And at the moment, these conversations are not nearly com-mon enough in organizations.

It's not always appropriate to be having a conversation with this focus. Often enough, having only a project-focused conver-sation is exactly the right thing to do.

## Putting the 3Ps to Use

"What's on your mind?" you ask.

"The [insert name of thing they're working on]," they say.

"So there are three different facets of that we could look at," you offer. "The *project* side—any challenges around the actual content. The *people* side—any issues with team members/ colleagues/other departments/bosses/customers/clients. And *patterns*—if there's a way that you're getting in your own way, and not showing up in the best possible way. Where should we start?"

It doesn't matter which one they pick—it will be a strong start to the conversation. And when they're done discussing that P, you can just take them to one of the other two Ps and ask, "If this was a thing, what would the challenge here be for you?"

And you'll likely have a deeper, more robust and richer conversation.

## Build Your New Habit Here

. . . . . . . . . . . . . . . . . . . . . . . . . . . .

WHEN THIS HAPPENS...

*Write out the moment, the person and perhaps the feelings that are your trigger.*

.................................................................................

.................................................................................

.................................................................................

.................................................................................

.................................................................................

.................................................................................

The typical trigger for this question is the start of some sort of conversation. Your direct report pops into your office for some advice. A customer calls you up. Your boss summons you into her office. A colleague sits down with you at lunch and asks if you have ten minutes to talk. You have a regular one-to-one with someone on your team. You're feeling anxious because the conversation hasn't really got started even though it's been going for a while. The trigger could even be an email or instant message from someone.

INSTEAD OF...

*Write out the old habit you want to stop doing. Be specific.*

.......................................................................................

.......................................................................................

.......................................................................................

.......................................................................................

.......................................................................................

The old habit could be doing small talk and more small talk, moving straight into advice-giving mode, defaulting to the standard agenda or telling the person what the topic of conversation is. It's likely to be something that's less about curiosity and more about your controlling the direction of the conversation.

I WILL...

*Describe your new habit.*

.......................................................................................

.......................................................................................

.......................................................................................

.......................................................................................

.......................................................................................

It's likely to sound a lot like, "I will ask them, 'What's on your mind?'" If the trigger comes in the form of an email or IM, you're allowed to just send a question in reply.

**WATCH IT WORK**

Watch the short videos at **TheCoachingHabit.com/videos** to deepen your learning and help turn insight into action.

**STARTING STRONG** "What's on your mind?" is a terrific opening question, but it's not the only one. In this video, Michael shares other options for starting your conversations more strongly and more quickly.

●   ●   ●

## FROM THE BOX OF CRAYONS LAB

"What's on your mind?" is the Facebook question. Or at least, it was. And then it wasn't for a while, as it was removed as the prompt. And then, soon after, it was the question again. I'm guessing Mark Zuckerberg and his team figured out that this question was the best they had.

So it's a question that's used by tens of millions of people every day to cue reflection and sharing. When we asked

Lindsay, our Box of Crayons researcher, to dig into the science behind why the question works so well, she directed us to one of the fundamental truths that neuroscience has laid bare: we are what we give our attention to. If we're mindful about our focus, so much the better. But if we're unwittingly distracted or preoccupied, we pay a price.

A 2010 study started by making the point that any time we have something on our mind, it's literally using up energy—even though it accounts for only about 2 percent of your body weight, your brain uses about 20 percent of your energy.

But more than that, what you're holding in your mind will unconsciously influence what you can notice and focus on. When you're thinking of buying a red Mazda, you suddenly start noticing all the red Mazdas on the road. Whatever you're thinking about can also influence the choices you make, so you might not, in fact, make the optimal choice.

Asking the Kickstart Question works as a little pressure-release valve and helps makes explicit something that might be unduly influencing the way you work. The question releases the challenge from where it may well be rattling around in a slightly unformed and unclear way that is, unbeknownst to you, narrowing the way you're seeing the world.

# Question
# Masterclass
# Part 2

# Cut the Intro and **Ask the Question**

There's an Internet meme about the best opening scene in a James Bond movie.

For some people, it's Roger Moore skiing off a cliff and then parachuting away (with a Union Jack–emblazoned parachute, naturally) in *The Spy Who Loved Me*.

For others, it's the more gritty black-and-white moment in *Casino Royale* when Daniel Craig gets his 00 accreditation by notching up his second kill.

My favourite? When Pierce Brosnan bungee-jumps off a massive dam in *GoldenEye*.

In any case, you'll notice a pattern here. No James Bond movie starts off slowly.

Pow! Within ten seconds you're into the action, the adrenaline has jacked and the heart is beating faster.

That's a stark contrast to the way many of us ask a question, which often has a slow, rambling, meandering introduction that feels more like the thousand and one nights of Scheherazade than anything Ian Fleming dreamt up.

Cut the preliminary flim-flam. You don't need a runway to pick up speed—you can just take off.

# If you know what question to ask, get to the point and **ask it**.

(And if you must have a lead-in phrase, try "Out of curiosity." It lessens the "heaviness" of any question and makes it easier to ask and answer.)

## Here's Your New Habit

WHEN THIS HAPPENS...

When I've got a question to ask...

INSTEAD OF...

Setting it up, framing it, explaining it, warming up to it and generally taking forever to get to the moment...

I WILL...

Ask the question. (And then shut up to listen to the answer.)

1 The Kickstart Question
What's on your mind?

**2 The AWE Question**

3 The Focus Question

4 The Foundation Question

5 The Lazy Question

6 The Strategic Question

7 The Learning Question

# 2: The AWE Question

In which the **Best Coaching Question in the World** is revealed and you marvel at the power of **three short words**.

## Real Magic

**B**eing a bad amateur magician makes me appreciate the real ones even more. You've probably seen the trick in which the magician is holding up her hand and seems to be producing a coin out of the ether. And then another. And then another. And then, if you're watching a certain Penn and Teller video on YouTube, a glint of goldfish. (Google "Masters of Magic Penn and Teller, Amazing tricks" to see what I mean. Google "collective noun for goldfish" if you're wondering what a glint is.)

I can't do that trick, not even close. But I can offer you a question that's so good we've actually considered trademarking it as The Best Coaching Question in the World, and it does something similar.

## The AWE Question: "And What Else?"

I know they seem innocuous. Three little words. But "**A**nd **W**hat **E**lse?"—the AWE Question—has magical properties.

With seemingly no effort, it creates more—more wisdom, more insights, more self-awareness, more possibilities—out of thin air.

There are three reasons it has the impact that it does: more options can lead to better decisions; you rein yourself in; and you buy yourself time.

## You Channel Your Inner Ron

If you've ever watched television in the last seventy years, you'll have bumped into Billy Mays, Vince Offer or Ron Popeil. They were TV pitch artists selling you the best dicer, grater, cleaning product or mop-up towel that $19.99 (plus shipping and handling) could buy. Ron Popeil is the grandfather of them all, and his stock phrase was "But wait, there's more..."

While no one here needs you to buy the ShamWow, you do want to remember that the first answer someone gives you is almost never the only answer, and it's rarely the best answer. You may think that's obvious, but it's less so than you realize.

Chip and Dan Heath, in their excellent book *Decisive: How to Make Better Choices in Life and Work,* quote a study by Paul Nutt, a man "who may know more than anyone alive about how managers make decisions." Using a rigorous protocol, he reviewed the outcomes of 168 decisions made within organizations. He found that in 71 percent of the decisions, the choice preceding the decision was binary. It was simply: Should we do this? Or should we not?

Nutt made the point that this percentage was on par with (actually, slightly worse than) the ability of teenagers to create options before making decisions. Yes, those terrible decisions teenagers tend to make. And at least teenagers have the excuse that their brains aren't yet fully formed. It's thus no surprise that Nutt found that decisions made from these binary choices had a failure rate greater than 50 percent.

He then looked at the success rate of decisions that involved more choices. For instance, what would happen if you added just one more option: Should we do this? *Or this*? Or not? The results were startling. Having at least one more option lowered the failure rate by almost half, down to about 30 percent.

When you use "And what else?" you'll get more options and often better options. Better options lead to better decisions. Better decisions lead to greater success.

## You Tame the Advice Monster

If this were a haiku rather than a book, it would read:

Tell less and ask more.
Your advice is not as good
As you think it is.

But seventeen syllables or not, this is easier said than done. We've all got a deeply ingrained habit of slipping into the advice-giver/expert/answer-it/solve-it/fix-it mode. That's no surprise, of course. When you take the premium that your organization places on answers and certainty, then blend in the increased sense of overwhelm and uncertainty and anxiety that many of us feel as our jobs and lives become more complex, and then realize that our brains are wired to have a strong preference for clarity and certainty, it's no wonder that we like to give advice. Even if it's the wrong advice—and it often is—giving it feels more comfortable than the ambiguity of asking a question.

In our training programs, we call this urge the Advice Monster. You have the best of intentions to stay curious and ask a few good questions. But in the moment, just as you are moving to that better way of working, the Advice Monster leaps out of the darkness and hijacks the conversation. Before you realize what's happening, your mind is turned towards finding The Answer and you're leaping in to offer ideas, suggestions and recommended ways forward.

There's a place for giving advice, of course. This book isn't suggesting that you never give anyone an answer ever again. But it's an overused and often ineffective response.

An intriguing (albeit difficult) exercise is to watch yourself and see how quickly you get triggered into wanting to give advice. Give yourself a day (or half a day, or an hour) and see how many times you are ready and willing to provide the answer. A much-quoted 1984 study by Howard Beckman and Richard Frankel found that the average time to interruption for doctors was eighteen seconds. And while we can all roll our eyes and say "those doctors," I've seen plenty of managers and leaders who bat a similar average.

In short, even though we don't really know what the issue is, or what's going on for the person, we're quite sure we've got the answer she needs.

Even though we don't really know what the issue is, **we're quite sure we've got the answer they need.**

"And what else?" breaks that cycle. When asking it becomes a habit, it's often the simplest way to stay lazy and stay curious. It's a self-management tool to keep your Advice Monster under restraints.

### You Buy Yourself Some Time

This is a secret. Just between you and me. As I'm sure I must have mentioned and PUT IN CAPS and underlined in my bio somewhere in this book, I was the first Canadian Coach of the Year. So I'm whispering this to you as a professional, respected and decorated coach.

When you're not entirely sure what's going on, and you need just a moment or two to figure things out, asking "And what else?" buys you a little extra time.

But that's on the down-low. Don't tell anyone else.

## Four Practical Tips for Asking "And What Else?"

To make sure the magic of AWE happens, follow a few simple guidelines:

### Stay Curious, Stay Genuine

Just because you've now got a fabulous question to use, that doesn't mean you can slip into a bored groove when asking it.

As you build this habit, don't just practice asking "And what else?" Use Dan Coyle's principles of Deep Practice from the chapter on habit building and get used to asking the question with genuine interest and curiosity. For bonus points, practice listening to the answers.

## Ask It One More Time

Hear an interview with DAN COYLE at the Great Work Podcast.

Let's start with the understanding that as a general rule, people ask this question too few times rather than too many. And the way to master this habit is to try it out and experiment and see what works. As a guideline, I typically ask it at least three times, and rarely more than five.

## Recognize Success

At some stage of the conversation, someone's going to say to you, "There *is* nothing else." When that happens, a perfectly reasonable reaction is a rapid heartbeat and slight panic.

Reframe that reaction as success. "There *is* nothing else" is a response you *should* be seeking. It means you've reached the end of this line of inquiry. Take a breath, take a bow and go on to another question.

## Move On When It's Time

If you can feel the energy going out of the conversation, you know it's time to move on from this angle. A strong "wrap it up" variation of "And what else?" is "Is there anything else?" That version of "And what else?" invites closure, while still leaving the door open for whatever else needs to be said.

"And what else?" is the quickest and easiest way to **uncover and create new possibilities**.

## Going Too Far: The Paradox of Choice

Options are good. The power of "And what else?" is that it's the quickest and easiest way to uncover and create new possibilities.

But having lots and lots and lots of options isn't always best.

Barry Schwartz, author of *The Paradox of Choice* (he gives a good TED Talk of the same name), brought to light a study of consumers in a grocery store. It was Jam Day, and one sample table had six varieties; the other, twenty-four. While the table with twenty-four types of jam was more popular, consumers sampling from the table of six flavours were ten times more likely to actually buy jam. The overwhelm of twenty-four flavours created decision-making paralysis.

Neuroscience has something useful to add to this conversation. The starting point for it was a 1956 paper by George A. Miller whose title tells you exactly what its conclusion was: "The Magical Number Seven, Plus or Minus Two: Some Limits on Our Capacity for Processing Information." Science has whittled that number down over time, so now it's generally assumed that four is actually the ideal number at which we can chunk information. In some ways, it's as if our unconscious brain counts like this: one, two, three, four... lots. That probably explains why we can remember the names of people in four-person bands, but not of those in bands of five or more.

So as you ask, "And what else?" the goal isn't to generate a bazillion options. It's to see what ideas that person already has (while effectively stopping you from leaping in with your own ideas). If you get three to five answers, then you've made great progress indeed.

## Finding the Right Moment

"And what else?" is such a useful question that you can add it into almost every exchange. For example:

- When you've asked someone, "What's on your mind?" and she answers, ask, "And what else?"

- When someone's told you about a course of action she intends to take, challenge her with "And what else could you do?"

- When you're trying to find the heart of the issue, and you ask, "What's the real challenge here for you?" and he offers up a timid or vague or insipid first answer, push deeper by asking, "And what else is a challenge here for you?"

- When you start your weekly check-in meeting by asking, "What's important right now?" keep the pressure on by asking, "And what else?"

- When someone's nudging a new idea to the fore, exploring new boundaries of courage and possibility, hold the space and deepen the potential by asking, "And what else might be possible?"

* When you're brainstorming new ideas and you don't want to get bogged down, keep the energy up by firing out, "And what else?"

## Build Your New Habit Here

. . . . . . . . . . . . . . . . . . . . . . . . . . . . .

WHEN THIS HAPPENS...

*Write out the moment, the person and perhaps the feelings that are your trigger.*

........................................................................

........................................................................

........................................................................

........................................................................

........................................................................

........................................................................

"And what else?" works so well because it keeps people generating options and keeps you shut up. So the trigger here is the opposite of that. It's when someone has given you an idea, when you want to give some advice, when you're sure you know the answer and are desperate to tell him or when he hasn't yet said, "There *is* nothing else!"

INSTEAD OF...

*Write out the old habit you want to stop doing. Be specific.*

...................................................................................

...................................................................................

...................................................................................

...................................................................................

The old habit will be largely about reverting to advice giving and moving into solution mode sooner than you need to. It could be: going with the first idea, or even the second idea or even the third idea; telling people the brilliant idea you've got before they've shared all their ideas; assuming you know the problem and/or the solution; or taking control and wrapping up the conversation.

I WILL...

*Describe your new habit.*

...................................................................................

...................................................................................

...................................................................................

...................................................................................

It's almost certainly something like, "I will ask them, 'And what else?'"

# ASK THE RIGHT QUESTIONS IF YOU'RE GOING TO **FIND THE RIGHT ANSWERS.**

Vanessa Redgrave

**WATCH IT WORK**

Watch the short videos at **TheCoachingHabit.com/videos** to deepen your learning and help turn insight into action.

**THE ONE QUESTION THAT RULES THEM ALL**  With a nod to J.R.R. Tolkien's *Lord of the Rings*, Michael delves into just why "And what else?" should be the first question you seek to master.

●   ●   ●

## FROM THE BOX OF CRAYONS LAB

If we're claiming that "And what else?" is the best coaching question in the world—and make no mistake, we are—then it's useful to understand the science behind the question. When we put the challenge to our researcher, Lindsay, she came back with a couple of compelling insights.

The first paper she cited has held up for more than eighty-five years since it was published in 1929. The study found that when students were offered a second pass at a number of true-or-false questions, this "deliberate reconsideration" helped students get more answers correct. These students performed better than a second set, who also got a second pass but didn't write down their answers during the first pass. This group performed worse than the first set of students. So it seems that committing to an answer and then having a chance to reflect on it creates greater accuracy. More recent studies have found that follow-up questions that promote higher-level thinking (like "And what else?") help deepen understanding and promote participation.

The second study Lindsay found involves psychologists picking on three-year-olds by getting them to do something naughty—peek at a toy—and then asking them if they'd peeked. About half of the kids who had peeked lied and denied doing it, only for most of them to immediately, accurately and revealingly answer the question, "What's the toy?" We're not that different from young kids. There's usually something else there waiting to be unearthed by the simple act of asking, and the AWE Question is one of the most effective ways of doing that.

# Question Masterclass Part 3

# Should You Ask **Rhetorical Questions?**

**W**hen Marlon Brando, his Godfather cheeks full of cotton wool, made someone an offer he couldn't refuse, it meant he'd wake up with a horse's head at the bottom of his bed.

You, of course, are a little more subtle about trying to get your way. You've taken on board that it's better for everyone if you give a little less advice and ask a few more questions. At the same time, in your heart you're pretty sure you know the answer to the problem being discussed. So you've mastered the fake question.

"Have you thought of...?"

"What about...?"

"Did you consider...?"

*Stop offering up advice with a question mark attached.* That doesn't count as asking a question.

If you've got an idea, wait. Ask, "And what else?" and you'll often find that the person comes up with that very idea that's burning a hole in your brain. And if she doesn't, then offer your idea—as an idea, not disguised as a fake question.

Stop offering up **advice** with a **question mark** attached.

## Here's Your New Habit

. . . . . . . . . . . . . . . . . . . . . . . . . .

WHEN THIS HAPPENS...

I've got the answer, which I want to suggest . . .

INSTEAD OF...

Asking a fake question such as "Have you thought of . . . ?" or "What about . . . ?" which is just advice with a question mark attached . . .

I WILL...

Ask one of the Seven Essential Questions. And if I want to present an idea, I'll offer it up as an option rather than a question.

1 The Kickstart Question
What's on your mind?

2 The AWE Question
And what else?

**3 The Focus Question**

4 The Foundation Question

5 The Lazy Question

6 The Strategic Question

7 The Learning Question

# 3: The Focus Question

In which you find out how to **stop spending so much time and effort solving the wrong problem.**

## Eureka. Kind Of.

. . . . . . . . . . . . . . . . . . . .

The world of science is full of accidental, brilliant discoveries. William Perkin was trying to cure malaria and ended up creating the first synthetic dye, mauveine. Andrew Fleming failed to tidy up his lab properly before heading off on vacation, and on his return found our first antibiotic, penicillin. The Post-it Note owes its success to a failed superglue. Viagra was originally created to deal with angina.

Sadly, this synchronicity is not what happens in your organization.

If your organizational culture is like every organizational culture I've ever seen (and it is), then it's a place that loves getting things done. Making it happen. Crossing it off the to-do list. And if you're like most of the managers I've ever worked with and for (and, for that matter, been), then you genuinely do want to figure it out.

The challenge is that with the years of conditioning you've had, as soon as you start hearing what a doctor might call "the presenting challenge," every fibre of your body is twitching with a desire to fix it, solve it, offer a solution to it. It's Pavlovian. Which is why people in organizations like yours around the world are working very hard and coming up with decent solutions to problems that just don't matter, and why the real challenges often go unaddressed.

When people start talking to you about the challenge at hand, what's essential to remember is that what they're laying out for you is rarely the actual problem. And when you start jumping in to fix things, things go off the rails in three ways: you work on the wrong problem; you do the work your team should be doing; and the work doesn't get done.

### You're Solving the Wrong Problem

You might have come up with a brilliant way to fix the challenge your team is talking about. However, the challenge they're talking about is most likely not the real challenge that needs to be sorted out. They could be describing any number of things: a symptom, a secondary issue, a ghost of a previous problem which is comfortably familiar, often even a half-baked solution to an unarticulated issue.

### You're Solving the Problem Yourself

Your team has trained you well to do their work for them. Any time there's a problem, rather than trying to figure it out themselves, they now come to you for the answer. It feels (at times

# Every fibre of your body is twitching with a desire to **fix it, solve it, offer a solution to it**.

. . . . . . . . . . . . . . . . . . . . . . . . . . . . . . . . . . . . . . . . . .

at least) as if it's easier that way for you and for them, but you may also be noticing that sense of overwhelm that comes from having to do your own job *and* some of the jobs of the others on your team. If you were in a therapist's office, at this stage the therapist would nod her head sagely and mutter "hmmm... co-dependent."

### You're Not Solving the Problem

It's not like you don't have your own work to do. And now you've found yourself responsible for solving everyone else's problems, too. And perhaps you don't actually have the answer to hand, so you ignore that email or you put it back in your in-tray or you make a vague promise about providing an answer in the near, but not too near, future. Suddenly you're stopping progress. Not only is the team overly dependent on you, but now you're feeling overwhelmed and you're slowing everything and everyone down. You've become the VP of Bottlenecking.

You need a way to manage the temptation to jump into fixing that opening challenge. You need to stop yourself (and your team) from getting entangled in the first problem that's put on the table. Slow down just a little and you'll get to the heart of the issue. And here's the question that makes all the difference:

## The Focus Question: What's the Real Challenge Here for You?

This is the question that will help slow down the rush to action, so you spend time solving the real problem, not just the first problem. It's no accident that it's phrased the way it is. Here's how it builds to become such a useful question:

Focus on the **real** problem, not the **first** problem.

- **What's the challenge?** Curiosity is taking you in the right direction, but phrased like this the question is too vague. It will most likely generate either an obvious answer or a somewhat abstract answer (or a combination of the two), neither of which is typically helpful.

- **What's the real challenge here?** Implied here is that there are a number of challenges to choose from, and you have to find the one that matters most. Phrased like this, the question will always slow people down and make them think more deeply.

- **What's the real challenge here for you?** It's too easy for people to pontificate about the high-level or abstract challenges in a situation. The "for you" is what pins the question to the person you're talking to. It keeps the question personal and makes the person you're talking to wrestle with her struggle and what she needs to figure out.

## How the Focus Question Cuts Through the Fog

Now that you know how the Focus Question is constructed, you'll see how it can cut through some of the well-practiced but ineffective patterns that show up between you and the person you're coaching. These are the patterns that keep things misty and vague when you're trying to bring the challenge into focus. At Box of Crayons, we call them the Foggy-fiers, and we call the three most common ones the Proliferation of Challenges, Coaching the Ghost, and Abstractions & Generalizations.

## Proliferation of Challenges

You've mastered the first of the Seven Essential Questions. You lean confidently in. "So," you ask, "what's on your mind?"

It comes tumbling out. "There's the website project—we've only been going for three weeks, and we're already a month behind. And Alberto's acting up again, confusing 'radio silence' for communication. We can't get any response from marketing about the launch, and I'm anxious about the budget for Project Tropic Thunder. And when I was driving in today, my engine started making this weird 'tock tock tock' sound…"

Now, if you've ever seen someone playing the Australian aboriginal instrument called the didgeridoo, you'll realize that the musician has an extraordinary ability to keep blowing out air without seeming to ever take a breath. Circular breathing means he can inhale through his nose while exhaling through his mouth. Try it. It feels impossible to do. But clearly not for this person. "What's on your mind?" has unleashed a seemingly unending stream of things he's worried about.

You may also have mastered the second of the Seven Essential Questions. But there's no way you're going to ask "And what else?" at this stage. You're already overwhelmed.

With every problem listed, you feel a little uptick of anxiety. Anxiety and satisfaction. Because with this many problems,

# WITHOUT A GOOD QUESTION, **A GOOD ANSWER HAS NO PLACE TO GO**.

Clayton Christensen

you're clearly in a position to help out in so many ways with a rich plethora of advice. The only question is where to start: with the first challenge mentioned, or with the one for which you're most confident about providing the answer.

Or—here's your new habit—none of the above. Instead of moving into advice-giving, solution-providing mode, you ask the Focus Question: "What's the real challenge here for you?"

### SYMPTOMS OF PROLIFERATION OF CHALLENGES

Have you ever made popcorn? One "pop." Then another. Then another. And then the popping goes crazy. Problems proliferate in the same way.

### SOLUTION TO PROLIFERATION OF CHALLENGES

Resist the temptation to do the work and to pick one of the many challenges as the starting point (even though, no doubt, you'll have an opinion on which one it should be). Instead, ask something like this:

"If you had to pick one of these to focus on, which one here would be the real challenge for you?"

## Coaching the Ghost

"What," you say with genuine curiosity, "is on your mind?"

"John."

"John?"

"John. He's a nightmare. Never before have I met someone who suffers more acutely from SOS: Shiny Object Syndrome. He's so scattered that it's like working with confetti."

"What? No! Tell me more," you encourage.

"And that's just the start of it. He has a very slippery relationship with truth and reality. It's not that he's lying exactly. It's just that the boundary between truth and not-truth are, well, there isn't one."

"O.M.G. And what else?"

"Ha! Did I tell you about the time when he ..."

And so it goes. A solid forty-five minutes talking about John. And no doubt it's a thoroughly entertaining conversation, at the end of which you both feel much better thanks to your inherent superiority over John and all his many flaws. And you feel like you've done some good coaching, because not only were you actively listening the whole time but you also bonded deeply.

This, however, is not coaching. Or managing. It's gossiping. Or, more bluntly, bitching and moaning.

The key thing to know here is that you can coach only the person in front of you. As tempting as it is to talk about a "third point" (most commonly another person, but it can also be a project or a situation), you need to uncover the challenge for the person to whom you're talking. So in the example above, it becomes a coaching conversation when it's a conversation about how this person is managing John, not a conversation about John.

And asking the Focus Question—"So what's the real challenge here for you?"—will get you there.

### SYMPTOMS OF COACHING THE GHOST

They're talking on and on about another person (complaining about the boss, going on about a customer interaction, worrying about someone on the team) or perhaps a project or a situation (complaining about the new processes, going on about the project creep, worrying about the impact of the business unit reorganization).

SOLUTION TO COACHING THE GHOST

Bring the focus back to the person you're talking to. Acknowledge what's going on, and ask the Focus Question. It will sound something like this:

"I think I understand some of what's going on with [insert name of the person or the situation]. What's the real challenge here for you?"

## Abstractions & Generalizations

You plunge in. "So what's on your mind?"

"I'm glad you asked. I don't know if you read the latest HBR blog post on this, but there's some interesting thoughts about the battle between strategy and culture. And I know this is something we're looking at as part of the project, and that the senior team is considering..."

You nod, sure she'll get to the point soon.

"Now, I think in general, the challenge with culture change is that there's a difference between what the leaders experience and what the rest of us experience. I heard it called 'the marathon effect,' which means the leadership crosses the line and 'finishes the race' before everyone else. Edgar Schein has some interesting things to say about it in his book..."

Your heart sinks a little. Maybe she's never going to get to the point.

It's not that this type of conversation isn't interesting, because quite often it is. It can feel more like a slightly academic discussion or an executive summary of what's going on. What's entirely unclear is how it is ever going to turn into one in which a problem gets identified and solved.

This is the time you need to ask the Focus Question: "So what's the real challenge here for you?"

### SYMPTOMS OF ABSTRACTIONS & GENERALIZATIONS

You're in the midst of a big-picture, high-level conversation about what's going on. It's almost as if the person talking isn't involved in it herself but is an observer. Quite often there's talk about "us" and "we," but there's no talk of "me" and "I."

### SOLUTION TO ABSTRACTIONS & GENERALIZATIONS

If you feel yourself drifting, you need to find a way to ground the challenge and connect it to the person you're talking to. Just as with Coaching the Ghost, it's about bringing the focus back to the person at hand. To do that, you'd ask something like this:

"I have a sense of the overall challenge. What's the real challenge here for you?"

## Moving from Performance to Development

In the Kickstart Question chapter, I touched briefly on the difference between coaching for performance and coaching for development. Coaching for performance is the label typically applied to everyday solving-the-problem management.

Coaching for development goes beyond just solving the problem and shifts the focus to the person who's trying to solve the problem. As I said, it's the difference between the fire and the person who's trying to put out the fire.

The simple act of adding "for you" to the end of as many questions as possible is an everyday technique for making conversations more development- than performance-oriented. Yes, the problems still get sorted out. But with "for you" there's often additional personal insight, and with personal insight comes increased growth and capability.

## Three Strategies to Make This Question Work for You

Now that you know why the Focus Question works so well, here are a few tips to ensure that it works well—for you.

### Trust That You're Being Useful

When you start shifting your behaviour from giving advice and providing solutions to asking questions, you will feel anxious. "I'm just asking questions. They're going to see right through this any minute now."

Learn to recognize the moment when you ask the question and there's a pause, a heartbeat of silence when you can see the person actually thinking and figuring out the answer. You can almost see new neural connections being made.

To further reassure yourself, master the last of the Seven Essential Questions—"What was most useful here for you?"— so you create a learning moment for the person and for you.

## Remember That There Is a Place for Your Advice

When someone pops his head around the door and asks, "Do you know where the folder is?" tell him where the folder is. Don't ask, "What's the real challenge here for you?" That's just annoying. (Although the upside might be that people stop interrupting you, so don't dismiss this tactic out of hand.) One of your roles as a manager and a leader is to have answers. We're just trying to slow down the rush to this role as your default behaviour.

## Remember the Second Question

Someone once said that everything tastes better with bacon. As a fallen vegetarian, I can attest to that. Equally, every question gets better when you add, "And what else?"

Asking, "What's the real challenge here for you?" Good.

Adding, "And what else? What else is a real challenge here for you?" Even better.

## Build Your New Habit Here

. . . . . . . . . . . . . . . . . . . . . . . . . . . .

WHEN THIS HAPPENS...

*Write out the moment, the person and perhaps the feelings that are your trigger.*

...................................................................

...................................................................

...................................................................

...................................................................

...................................................................

...................................................................

The pattern we're breaking here is overworking the wrong problem, so the trigger is any time you start to focus on a particular challenge. Coming up with ways to fix things feels more comfortable than sitting in the ambiguity of trying to figure out the challenge, but that's where the power of this question lies. So the trigger could be when your team is discussing a challenge or a project and the conversation has already moved to solutions, or when someone on your team is wrestling with a problem but you're not really sure if he knows what the challenge is, or when you're feeling scared or anxious or uncertain about a challenge you're facing.

INSTEAD OF...

*Write out the old habit you want to stop doing. Be specific.*

...................................................................

...................................................................

..........................................................................

..........................................................................

..........................................................................

The Foggy-fiers are the old habits you're trying to break. So the "instead of" here might be when you decide that the first challenge probably is the challenge; or when you leave the challenge a little high-level and abstract so people kinda know what it is, or so you assume; or when there are lots of challenges and you're trying to fix them all or they all seem equally important; or when the problem is someone else's problem (or just someone else); or when you spend no time on focusing on what the challenge truly is and move right to actions.

I WILL...

*Describe your new habit.*

..........................................................................

..........................................................................

..........................................................................

..........................................................................

..........................................................................

I'm pretty sure it will be, "Ask 'What's the real challenge here for you?'"

**WATCH IT WORK**

Watch the short videos at **TheCoachingHabit.com/videos** to deepen your learning and help turn insight into action.

**HOW TO HELP YOUR TEAM FIND FOCUS**   You'll find a number of questions and tools you can use to help your team find the focus they need to do more Great Work.

* * *

## FROM THE BOX OF CRAYONS LAB

When we set our researcher, Lindsay, onto the science behind this question, she came up with any number of studies on the value of helping people narrow their focus. You may remember me mentioning Barry Schwartz's *The Paradox of Choice* in a previous chapter, and there are multiple studies that show how limiting choices reduces overwhelm and polychronicity, a fancy word for multitasking. But there's more to this question than just providing the focus that will liberate creativity and unfreeze procrastination.

Part of what makes the Focus Question work so well are those two final words, "for you." A 1997 study involving a fairly convoluted series of math problems focused on the impact of having the word "you" as part of a math problem's description. The researchers found that when the word "you" was present, the questions needed to be repeated fewer times, and the problems were solved in a shorter amount of time and with more accuracy.

You can take this insight and add it to *all* of the questions you ask people. Adding "for you" to a question helps people figure out the answers faster and more accurately.

# Question
# Masterclass
# Part 4

# Stick to Questions Starting with "What"

**P**eter Senge was big in the 1990s when his book *The Fifth Discipline* and its theme of the learning organization caught the imagination of executives everywhere. One of the tools he introduced was called "The Five Whys," a self-explanatory process to work backwards through a story to find a root cause of "a pernicious, recurring problem."

Simon Sinek carried on that theme with his popular book, *Start with Why: How Great Leaders Inspire Everyone to Take Action* (he also has a great TED Talk). For Sinek, organizations must have as their foundation absolute clarity about the Why of their existence if they're going to inspire people—customers and employees both—to stay engaged with their brand.

Ignore both authors.

Yes, there's a place for asking "Why?" in organizational life. And no, it's not while you're in a focused conversation with the people you're managing. Here are two good reasons:

- **You put them on the defensive.** Get the tone even slightly wrong and suddenly your "Why...?" come across as "What the hell were you thinking?" It's only downhill from there.

- **You're trying to solve the problem.** You ask why because you want more detail. You want more detail because you want to fix the problem. And suddenly you're back in the vicious circles of overdependence and overwhelm.

# If you're not trying to fix things, **you don't need the backstory.**

*Stick to questions starting with "What" and avoid questions starting with "Why."* It's no accident that six of the Seven Essential Questions are What questions.

## Here's Your New Habit

. . . . . . . . . . . . . . . . . . . . . . . . . .

WHEN THIS HAPPENS...

When I'm tempted to ask them why...

INSTEAD OF...

Beginning the question with "Why..."

I WILL...

Reframe the question so it starts with "What." So, as some examples, instead of "Why did you do that?" ask "What were you hoping for here?" Instead of "Why did you think this was a good idea?" ask "What made you choose this course of action?" Instead of "Why are you bothering with this?" ask "What's important for you here?"

# An Irresistible 1-2-3 Combination

**The first three questions can combine** to become a robust script for your coaching conversation.

You'll be surprised and delighted at just how often these are exactly the right questions to ask.

Open with:
**What's on your mind?**
*The perfect way to start; the question is open but focused.*

Check in:
**Is there anything else on your mind?**
*Give the person an option to share additional concerns.*

Then begin to focus:
**So what's the real challenge here for you?**
*Already the conversation will deepen. Your job now is to find what's most useful to look at.*

Ask:
**And what else (is the real challenge here for you)?**
*Trust me, the person will have something. And there may be more.*

Probe again:
**Is there anything else?**
*You'll have most of what matters in front of you now.*

So get to the heart of it and ask:
**So ... what's the real challenge here for you?**

1 The Kickstart Question
What's on your mind?

2 The AWE Question
And what else?

3 The Focus Question
What's the real challenge here for you?

**4 The Foundation Question**

5 The Lazy Question

6 The Strategic Question

7 The Learning Question

# 4: The Foundation Question

In which the question that lies at the very **heart** of adult-to-adult relationships is discussed.

## How to Be a Grown-Up

Peter Block is a brilliant thinker about how we behave at work. His book *Flawless Consulting* should be on the bookcase's top shelf for anyone who's trying to get any thing done within organizations, as should *The Answer to How Is Yes*. I've heard him frame the work he does as "giving people the responsibility for their own freedom." That's a big statement that raises as many questions as it answers. One of those questions might be "What's freedom?" and Block would probably respond by saying that it is being able to show up as an adult in our work and being able to deal with those around us as adults, too.

## The Foundation Question: "What Do You Want?"

Taking responsibility for your own freedom is notoriously difficult to do. Block defined an adult-to-adult relationship as one in which you are "able to ask for what you want, knowing that the answer may be No." That's why at the heart of this book is this simple but potent question, "What do you want?" I sometimes call it the Goldfish Question because it often elicits that response: slightly bugged eyes, and a mouth opening and closing with no sound coming out. Here's why the question is so difficult to answer.

We often don't know what we actually want. Even if there's a first, fast answer, the question "But what do you *really* want?" will typically stop people in their tracks.

But even if you do know what you want, what you really really want, it's often hard to ask for it. We make up reasons about why it's not appropriate just now to make the request; it's because the timing's not right, or the person's only going to say No, or *Who are you anyway to make such a boldfaced ask?* What we want is often left unsaid.

But even if you know what you want and are courageous enough to ask for what you want, it's often hard to say it in a way that's clearly heard and understood. Sometimes the responsibility for that rests with you. You've found a way to hide what you want under layers of rhetoric; or been distracted from what you really want with various other, less important hopes; or trusted that the heavy hints you'd made were sufficient; or assumed that the slightly passive-aggressive comment was enough. Sometimes the responsibility for unheard requests rests with the people you're asking. They're pursuing their own agendas, or their confirmation bias means they hear something completely different from what you're saying, or they're fake-listening and not really paying attention at all.

But even if you know what you want, and you ask for what you want, and it seems to be heard, it's often hard to hear the answer to your request, which might be not *Yes* but rather *No*. Or *Maybe*. Or *Not that, but this instead*. And on the other side of the conversation, it can be hard to understand that when someone makes a request, when she tells you what she wants, you don't actually have to say *Yes*. You can say *No*. Or *Maybe*. Or *Not that, but this instead*.

You can see there are many reasons that the ship of "What do you want?" might never make it out of the harbour. George Bernard Shaw put it succinctly when he said, "The single biggest problem with communication is the illusion that it has taken place." The illusion that both parties to the conversation know what the other party wants is pervasive, and it sets the stage for plenty of frustrating exchanges.

Not all is lost, though. One of the ways to ensure smoother sailing is to understand the difference between wants and needs.

## Untangling Wants and Needs

When I first started getting an allowance—we called it "pocket money" in Australia—it came with a parental conversation about saving, and the difference between wants and needs. It's

The illusion that both parties to the conversation know what the other party wants is pervasive, **and it sets the stage for plenty of frustrating exchanges**.

a useful distinction, and I'd guess that a few seconds' reflection on the difference between wants and needs brings these descriptions to mind:

**Want:** I'd like to have this.
**Need:** I must have this.

That distinction makes plenty of sense in theory. In practice, it's hard to stop everything from just getting the upgrade to needs, which means that the distinction collapses in on itself. Marshall Rosenberg is the creator of Nonviolent Communication (NVC), a communication process that "helps people to exchange the information necessary to resolve conflicts and differences peacefully." In the NVC model, he gives the differences between wants and needs a more practical and sustainable twist.

In Rosenberg's model, wants are the surface requests, the tactical outcomes we'd like from a situation. A want could be anything from getting a report done by a certain date to understanding whether you need to attend a meeting or not. This kind of information is what typically shows up in response to our question, "What do you want?"

Needs go deeper, and identifying them helps you pull back the curtain to understand the more human driver who might be behind the want. Drawing on the work of economist Manfred Max-Neef, Rosenberg says that there are nine self-explanatory universal needs.

| AFFECTION | CREATION | RECREATION |
| --- | --- | --- |
| FREEDOM | IDENTITY | UNDERSTANDING |
| PARTICIPATION | PROTECTION | SUBSISTENCE |

When you ask someone, "What do you want?" listen to see if you can guess the need that likely lies behind the person's request. For example, when someone says, "I want you to talk to the VP for me," he might really be needing protection (I'm too junior) or participation (I need you to do your part in this project). When someone tells you, "I want to leave early today," she might really be asking for understanding (it's difficult at home) or creation (I need to go to my class). When someone says, "I want you to do a new version of the report," the base need might be freedom (I don't want to do it), identity (I want you to know I'm the boss here) or subsistence (my success depends on your getting this right.)

You can see that recognizing the need gives you a better understanding of how you might best address the want. And there's a flip side to that as well. As you frame your own request for what you want, see if you can articulate what the need is behind the request.

## Ask a Question. Trade Answers.

I was not a successful law student. I remember almost nothing from my classes, and I ended my studies by being sued by one of my lecturers for defamation. It's a long story.

But one thing that has stuck in my brain is that the essence of a legal contract is an exchange of value. It turns out that this principle can help you build more resilient and mutually beneficial relationships with the people with whom you work.

There are times when simply asking a question is the thing to do. And there are other times when sharing your answer to that same question can increase its impact. "What do you want?" is an extraordinarily strong question. Its power is amplified when you not only ask the question of the person you're working with but also answer the question for yourself. It takes us back to Peter Block's point, mentioned at the start of the chapter, about the nature of adult-to-adult conversations. When we each understand what the other wants, we're in the middle of an interesting and worthwhile conversation. And part of the reason for that is the neuroscience of engagement.

## Our New Frontier: The Neuroscience of Engagement

As we tap into our twenty-first-century laptops, one click on Google Earth shows that there's not a whole lot of *terra incognito* left. You can visit any country you want, and a few intrepid people have even visited all 195.

But there are still new frontiers of knowledge to be explored, and one of the most exciting is neuroscience, the study of the brain. Using creative experiments and sophisticated technology, such as fMRI and EEG machines, we're starting to see that the art of leadership has its basis in science. We can now begin to see what really works and what doesn't work in our attempts to engage with those we manage and influence.

As we're at the heart of this book with this, the Foundation Question, now is a perfect time to make the connection between your coaching habit and your head by looking at the neuroscience of engagement.

## Five Times a Second

The "fundamental organizing principle of the brain"—neuroscientist Evan Gordon's words—is the risk-and-reward response. Five times a second, at an unconscious level, your brain is scanning the environment around you and asking itself: Is it safe here? Or is it dangerous?

It likes safe, of course. When your brain feels safe, it can operate at its most sophisticated level. You're more subtle in your thinking, better able to see and manage ambiguity. You assume positive intent of those around you, and you're able to tap collective wisdom. You're engaged and you're moving forward.

Five times a second, your brain is scanning the environment and asking itself: **Is it safe here? Or is it dangerous?**

# WHEN WILL THE **RHETORICAL QUESTIONS** END?

George Carlin

When the brain senses danger, there's a very different response. Here it moves into the familiar fight-or-flight response, what some call the "amygdala hijack." Things get black and white. Your assumption is that "they" are against you, not with you. You're less able to engage your conscious brain, and you're metaphorically, and most likely literally, backing away.

And it's not a balanced decision. For obvious evolutionary reasons, we're biased to assume that situations are dangerous rather than not. We may not be right, but over the course of humankind's evolution, the successful survival strategy has been "better to be safe than sorry."

In other words, if you're not sure about a situation, you'll default to reading it as unsafe. And start backing away.

## Wait, Come Back!

And there's the challenge for you as a busy and ambitious manager. You want those you interact with—your team, your boss, your customers, your suppliers—to be engaging rather than retreating. You want your people to feel that working with you is a place of reward, not risk. And you also realize that *you* want to feel like you're safe so that you can stay at your smartest, rather than in fight-or-flight mode.

So how do you influence others' brains and your own so that situations are read as rewarding, not risky?

There are four primary drivers—they spell out the acronym TERA—that influence how the brain reads any situation. TERA is a handy acronym, as it brings to mind "terroir"—the influence that a specific location has on the taste of the wine made from the grapes grown there. When you focus on TERA, you're thinking about how you can influence the environment that drives engagement.

* **T is for tribe.** The brain is asking, "Are you with me, or are you against me?" If it believes that you're on its side, it increases the TERA Quotient. If you're seen as the opposition, the TERA Quotient goes down.

* **E is for expectation.** The brain is figuring out, "Do I know the future or don't I?" If what's going to happen next is clear, the situation feels safe. If not, it feels dangerous.

* **R is for rank.** It's a relative thing, and it depends not on your formal title but on how power is being played out in the moment. "Are you more important or less important than I am?" is the question the brain is asking, and if you've diminished my status, the situation feels less secure.

* **A is for autonomy.** Dan Pink talks about the importance of this in his excellent book *Drive*. "Do I get a say or don't I?" That's the question the brain is asking as it gauges the degree of autonomy you have in any situation. If you believe you do have a choice, then this environment is more likely to be a place of reward and therefore engagement. If you believe you don't have a choice so much, then it becomes less safe for you.

Your job is to increase the TERA Quotient whenever you can. That's good for the person you're speaking with, and it's good for you. Asking questions in general, and asking "What do you want?" specifically, will do that.

It increases the sense of tribe-iness, as, rather than dictating what someone should do, you're helping him solve a challenge. And in doing so, you're increasing not only his sense of autonomy—you're assuming that he can come up with answers and encouraging him to do so—but his rank as well, because you're letting him "have the floor" and go first. The question "What do you want?" strongly affects the drivers of rank and autonomy. Expectation, the other factor, may be a little depressing (a question contains more ambiguity than an answer), but that's OK. Your goal is to raise the overall TERA Quotient, and by asking questions you do just that.

## Build Your New Habit Here

WHEN THIS HAPPENS...

*Write out the moment, the person and perhaps the feelings that are your trigger.*

.................................................................................

.................................................................................

.................................................................................

.................................................................................

.................................................................................

The trigger for this habit is when you or he or the conversation feels a little stuck. You may be circling through options and none of them feel quite right or exciting or engaging. It can also be when he is procrastinating on taking action (or you are), and you're not sure why. Or it can be any time you're in a slightly fraught conversation with someone—someone on your team, your boss, a customer, a vendor. Perhaps the conversation goes off the rails and hasn't really got started and you're wondering how to get things back on track.

INSTEAD OF...
*Write out the old habit you want to stop doing.*

...................................................................................

...................................................................................

...................................................................................

...................................................................................

...................................................................................

The trap of the old habit is that you think you know what they want. And sometimes, they think they know what they want. So the "instead of..." here is when you're pretty sure you know what they want but haven't actually asked them, or when you keep going even though you think you're missing something. Or when you try to impose your idea, or your opinion, or your course of action. Or when you're stuck and not taking action on something and you're not sure why.

I WILL...

*Describe your new habit.*

...............................................................................

...............................................................................

...............................................................................

...............................................................................

...............................................................................

...............................................................................

It's simple. Ask "What do you want?" For bonus points, tell the person what you want as well.

**WATCH IT WORK**

Watch the short videos at **TheCoachingHabit.com/videos** to deepen your learning and help turn insight into action.

**THE TERA QUOTIENT** See how to translate the neuroscience of engagement into tactics and behaviours that will help you and others stay engaged.

## FROM THE BOX OF CRAYONS LAB

When I asked Lindsay, our researcher, to dig into the question "What do you want?" she took me into the world of psychotherapy. And I went there reluctantly. Therapy in its many forms can of course be an extraordinarily effective intervention, but it doesn't typically have a place as a tool for managers to wield in their organizational lives.

However, there's insight to be gleaned here from a school of therapy known as "solution-based" therapy. They have a go-to question called the miracle question. Several variations exist, but in essence it's this: "Suppose that tonight, while you're sleeping, a miracle happens. When you get up in the morning tomorrow, how will you know that things have suddenly got better?"

The miracle question helps people to more courageously imagine what better (and *much* better) really looks like. A 10× improvement, not a 10 percent tweak. But I think that much of its genius is that it also deliberately focuses on the end before the means. In other words, start with the end in mind rather than (as often happens) collapsing the "what" of the outcome with the "how" of the next steps and immediately getting discouraged.

The Foundation Question—"What do you want?"—is direct, rather than indirect. But it has the same effect of pulling people to the outcome, and once you see the destination, the journey often becomes clearer.

# Question
# Masterclass
# Part 5

# Get Comfortable with Silence

**W**hen you ask someone one of the Seven Essential Questions, sometimes what follows is silence.

Echoing, endless silence.

And by "endless" I mean sometimes as long as three or four seconds.

In those moments, as everything slows to *Matrix*-style "bullet time," every part of you is desperate to fill the void.

Put this existential angst aside. Silence is often a measure of success.

It may be that the person you're coaching is the type who needs a moment or three to formulate the answer in his head before speaking it. In which case you're giving him that space.

Or it may be that, like me, he's the type who typically just launches into an answer without knowing what he's going to say.

In either case, it means he's thinking, searching for the answer. He's creating new neural pathways, and in doing so literally increasing his potential and capacity.

*Bite your tongue, and don't fill the silence.* I know it will be uncomfortable, and I know it creates space for learning and insight.

# Silence is often a measure of success.

## Here's Your New Habit

WHEN THIS HAPPENS...

When I've asked a question and she doesn't have an answer ready within the first two seconds...

INSTEAD OF...

Filling up the space with another question or the same question just asked a new way or a suggestion or just pointless words...

I WILL...

Take a breath, stay open and keep quiet for another three seconds.

1 The Kickstart Question
What's on your mind?

2 The AWE Question
And what else?

3 The Focus Question
What's the real challenge here for you?

4 The Foundation Question
What do you want?

**5 The Lazy Question**

6 The Strategic Question

7 The Learning Question

# 5: The Lazy Question

In which you discover the question that will make you more useful to those you manage, while working less hard, and **you decide that being lazy is a good thing after all**.

## You're So..."Helpful"

**Y**ou're a good person, and you're doing your very best to let your people thrive. You want to "add value" and be useful. You like to feel that you're contributing. However, there's being helpful, and then there's being "helpful," as in stepping in and taking over. And way too often, you get suckered into doing the latter. Then everyone—you, the person you're "helping," the organization—pays a price for your attempted helpfulness. Your good intentions often end up contributing to a relentless cycle of exhaustion, frustration and, ironically, reduced impact.

Edgar Schein has untangled the paradox of being helpful in his excellent book *Helping*. At its crux is the insight that when you offer to help someone, you "one up" yourself: you raise your status and you lower hers, whether you mean to or not. This idea seems counterintuitive, I know, because so often our desire to help comes from genuine caring. But the insight rings true when you put yourself in the shoes of the person who is being offered help. When you think back to times when "help" has been thrust upon you, you'll probably notice a curious mixture of reactions that include resistance, frustration, dis-empowerment and annoyance.

So what's going on? And how can you temper your approach so that more often you are helpful in a way that actually helps? A useful starting point happens to be a triangle.

## The (New) Seven Dwarfs & the Karpman Drama Triangle

Transactional Analysis (TA) is the slightly-out-of-fashion thera-peutic model that has given us the labels of "parent-child" and "adult-adult." It's intriguing, but almost impossible to apply directly in organizations. It involves too much therapy-speak. The Drama Triangle, a practical interpretation of TA developed by Stephen Karpman, is one way to make TA practical and useful.

The Drama Triangle starts by assuming that, at least some of the time, we're playing less-than-fantastic versions of ourselves with most of the people with whom we interact. If you've ever found yourself playing one of the Seven Dysfunctional Dwarfs (Sulky, Moany, Shouty, Crabby, Martyr-y, Touchy and Petulant), even when you know you should know better, you get the point.

When this happens, Karpman says, we're bouncing around between three archetypal roles—Victim, Persecutor and Res-cuer—each one as unhelpful and dysfunctional as the other. As you read the descriptions of each role below, do two things: bring to mind someone who's particularly adept at each role, and bring to mind the circumstances in which you most commonly play each role.

## Victim

**The core belief:** "My life is so hard; my life is so unfair. 'Poor me.'"

**The dynamic:** "It's not my fault (it's theirs)."

**The benefits of playing the role:** You have no responsibility for fixing anything; you get to complain; you attract Rescuers.

**The price paid for playing the role:** You have no sense of being able to change anything—any change is outside your control. You're known to be ineffective. And no one likes a whiner.

**Stuck is:** "I feel stuck because I have no power and no influence. I feel useless."

## Persecutor

**The core belief:** "I'm surrounded by fools, idiots or just people less good than me."

**The dynamic:** "It's not my fault (it's yours)."

**The benefits of playing the role:** You feel superior and have a sense of power and control.

**The price paid for playing the role:** You end up being responsible for everything. You create Victims. You're known as a micromanager. People do the minimum for you and no more. And no one likes a bully.

**Stuck is:** "I feel stuck because I don't trust anyone. I feel alone."

### Rescuer

**The core belief:** "Don't fight, don't worry, let me jump in and take it on and fix it."

**The dynamic:** "It's my fault/responsibility (not yours)."

**The benefits of playing the role:** You feel morally superior; you believe you're indispensable.

**The price paid for playing the role:** People reject your help. You create Victims and perpetuate the Drama Triangle. And no one likes a meddler.

**Stuck is:** "I feel stuck because my rescuing doesn't work. I feel burdened."

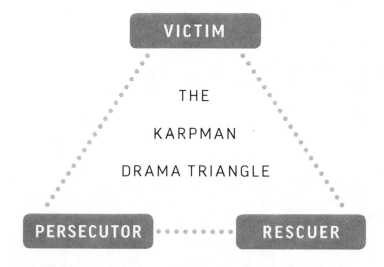

These three labels aren't descriptions of who you are. They're descriptions of how you're behaving in a given situation. No one is inherently a Victim or a Persecutor or a Rescuer. They are roles we end up playing when we've been triggered and, in that state, find a less-than-effective version of ourselves playing out.

## "All the World's a Stage . . ."

We all play all of these roles all the time. Often, we'll cycle through all of the roles in a single exchange with someone, lurching from Victim to Rescuer to Persecutor and back again. To make the point, here's a made-up conversation I might recently have had with a client after I gave a speech.

**Me** [shouty]: This room setup is all wrong! I sent through my demands of how I want this; how hard is it just to set up the room as requested? And donuts. Stop feeding people donuts. And the session starts in fifteen minutes! (Persecutor)

**Client** [whiny]: I sent the setup sheet to the logistics people, but it's really hard to get them to respond and I've had to organize this whole conference by myself without any support and . . . (Victim)

**Me** [resigned]: Look, don't worry about it, I'll just rearrange the room by myself and get the tech set up. And I'll cook eggs for everyone. (Rescuer)

**Client** [frustrated]: This is just typical of prima donna speakers like you; we're paying you too much already and you have to have everything "just so" and then you take over any time you're not happy. (Persecutor)

**Me** [whiny]: I'm just trying to make sure my session's a good one; no one understands how hard it is to get a room set up the right way, and then as soon as you try, everyone hates you. (Victim)

And so it goes.

And it can happen even faster than that. Think of the most annoying person on your team right now, the one who's giving you difficulty even as we speak. Did you notice that in a flash, you jumped to Persecutor (They make me so mad!), Victim (It's not fair, why can't I get them onto someone else's team?) and Rescuer (I'll just keep trying to do their work for them until they get up to speed) all at once?

## Your Go-to Role

That said, we tend to have a favourite role that we default to most of the time. If you're like the majority of the people I've taught, when asked to identify which of these roles you play most often, you'll choose the Rescuer. And even if Rescuer is not your default role, I'm betting you recognize it well enough.

# THE MINUTE WE BEGIN TO THINK WE HAVE ALL THE ANSWERS, **WE FORGET THE QUESTIONS.**

Madeleine L'Engle

When we're in Rescuer mode, we're constantly leaping in to solve problems, jumping in to offer advice, taking over responsibilities that others should rightfully keep for themselves. We do it with good intentions; we're just trying to help, to "add value" as managers. But you can already see the price that's being paid by both sides. You're exhausted—and they're irritated. You're limiting opportunities for growth and for expanding the potential of those you're working with. More provocatively, you might be coming to understand that Rescuers create Victims, though we want to believe that it's the other way around (which is also true, but not only true).

## Are You Doomed? (Yes, You're Doomed)

Seeing the pattern of the Drama Triangle is a strong first step in breaking the working-too-hard pattern of the time-crunched manager. Once you understand the triggers, you can start to reshape the habit.

The bad news is that you are in fact destined to keep falling into the Drama Triangle for the rest of your life.

The good news is that you'll get better and better at recognizing it and breaking the pattern, faster and more often.

Samuel Beckett put it best: "Go on failing. Go on. Only next time, try to fail better."

You'll fail better by recognizing more quickly that you're in the Drama Triangle and by asking the Lazy Question—"How can I help?"—to pull yourself out of the triangle faster.

## The Lazy Question: How Can I Help?

The power of "How can I help?" is twofold. First, you're forcing your colleague to make a direct and clear request. That may be useful to him. He might not be entirely sure why he started this conversation with you. Sure, he knows he wants something, but until you asked the question, he didn't know that he wasn't exactly clear on what he wanted. Unless he was, in which case the question is useful for you, because now you can decide whether you want to honour the request.

Second (and possibly even more valuably), it stops you from thinking that you know how best to help and leaping into action. That's the classic Rescuer behaviour. Like "And what else?" this question is a self-management tool to keep you curious and keep you lazy. Too much of your day is spent doing things you think people want you to do. Sometimes you're completely off base, but that's not the worst of it because that gets sorted out relatively quickly. More dangerous is when you're only slightly wrong. That's when you find yourself kind of doing what they want, but not enough so it's really useful, and not so wrong that someone tells you to stop.

## Be Blunt...

The more direct version of "How can I help?" is "What do you want from me?" If "How can I help?" is James Bond in a tuxedo, then "What do you want from me?" is Bond in bust-out-of-the-baddies'-evil-lair mode. It strips the conversation down to understanding the essential exchange: What do you want? What do I want? And now, what shall we do about that?

## ... But Be Careful

You can likely guess that how "What do you want from me?" lands will depend in no small part on the tone of voice in which it's asked. To connect it to the Drama Triangle, if you're in Persecutor mode, it might come across as aggressive; in Victim mode, as whiny; and in Rescuer mode, as smothering.

A way to soften this question, as with all questions, is to use the phrase "Out of curiosity." What that does is shift the question from perhaps coming across as an inquisition to being a more noble inquiry. Other phrases that can have a similar softening effect on the question being asked are "Just so I know..." or "To help me understand better..." or even "To make sure that I'm clear..."

## The Anxiety of Asking "How Can I Help?" & How to Manage It

The biggest worry people have about asking, "How can I help?" is the range of potential answers:

- "I need you to do this horrible/unreasonable/impossible task."

- "I'd like you to have the difficult conversation I'm avoiding."

- "Can you please give me all of your budget?"

• "Here's one extra thing for your already towering pile of responsibilities."

What's essential to realize is that regardless of the answer you receive, you have a range of responses available to you.

"Yes" is one, of course. You can always say Yes. But you don't have to say Yes, and your sense of obligation to say Yes is the source of your anxiety.

"No, I can't do that" is another option. Having the courage to say No is one of the ways you stop being so "helpful."

"I can't do that... but I could do [insert your counteroffer]" is a nice middle ground. Don't just give them a No; give them some other choices.

And finally, you can just buy yourself some time. "Let me think about that." "I'm not sure—I'll need to check a few things out."

## Avoid the Rescuer Sucker Punch with This New Habit

It's hard enough, when someone starts telling you what's going on, to resist moving into advice-giving, solution-providing mode. It feels nearly impossible when someone asks you a question that's a direct appeal for your advice: "How do I...?" or "What do you think I should do about...?" Seductive and

"What do you think I should do about...?" is **the cheddar on the mousetrap.**

dangerous, this is the cheddar on the mousetrap, the light on the mosquito zapper, the block of chocolate in the cupboard. Before you know what's happening, you're giving an answer.

Now, there's a time and a place for giving advice. The goal here *isn't* to avoid ever providing an answer. But it is to get better at having people find their own answers. So here's your new habit:

WHEN THIS HAPPENS...

Someone gives you a call/drops by your cubicle/shouts out across the office/sends you a text message and asks, "How do I [insert query most likely to sucker you in]?"

INSTEAD OF...

Giving her the answer...

I WILL...

Say, "That's a great question. I've got some ideas, which I'll share with you. But before I do, what are your first thoughts?"

And when she answers, which she will, you'll nod your head and be engaged and interested, and when she finishes, say, "That's terrific. What else could you do?"

More nodding, more being interested.

Then say, "This is all good. Is there anything else you could try here?"

And then, and only then, you can add your own idea into the mix if you wish. And of course, if the conversation is going well, keep asking "And what else?" until she has run out of ideas.

## Build Your New Habit Here

WHEN THIS HAPPENS...

*Write out the moment, the person and perhaps the feelings that are your trigger.*

...........................................................................

...........................................................................

...........................................................................

...........................................................................

...........................................................................

...........................................................................

The trigger here is how much you want to help. So what sets you off? It's likely when someone asks, "How do I...?" or "Could you...?" or "What's the way to...?" Or perhaps it's just when someone comes into your office and tells you about a situation, and the perfect solution pops immediately into your mind. Or when that happens in a team meeting. Or when you think to yourself, *It's faster to do this myself,* even though you're unclear on what the "this" really is. In short, it's every time you get that urge to jump in, help out and volunteer. And the real insult here—to your time, effort and good intentions—is that the recipients may not even want or need what you're about to give them.

INSTEAD OF...

*Write out the old habit you want to stop doing. Be specific.*

...........................................................................................

...........................................................................................

...........................................................................................

...........................................................................................

...........................................................................................

...........................................................................................

The old habit you're breaking is your jumping into helpful, action mode. You're giving the solution, you're providing the answer, you're adding something to your to-do list. You're assuming you know what the request is, even though the request hasn't been clearly made. In short, you're taking responsibility.

I WILL....

*Describe your new habit. It's likely to be some version of "I will ask them, 'How can I help?'"*

...........................................................................................

...........................................................................................

...........................................................................................

..................................................................

..................................................................

..................................................................

..................................................................

..................................................................

You're seeking clarity by asking, "How can I help?" Or you're being even blunter and asking, "What do you want from me?"

**WATCH IT WORK**

Watch the short videos at **TheCoachingHabit.com/videos** to deepen your learning and help turn insight into action.

**HOW TO BE MORE HELPFUL (RATHER THAN "HELPFUL")**
Michael unpacks the work of Edgar Schein to help deepen our understanding of why often our best attempts to be helpful generate resistance and end in failure.

**THE DRAMA TRIANGLE RECAP**  If learning about the Drama Triangle struck a chord with you, then these videos will help you learn more and share the wisdom with others.

## FROM THE BOX OF CRAYONS LAB

In the "And what else?" chapter, we mentioned a study that found that the average time a doctor waited to interrupt his or her patients was a mere eighteen seconds. But our Box of Crayons researcher has found some other studies that show us that not all doctors lack conversational graces.

Lindsay uncovered a study about different approaches to beginning a conversation with a patient. Some doctors used a more general inquiry, such as, "How can I help?" Others used more confirmatory questions, such as "I understand you're having some sinus problems today?" With the more general inquiries, patients gave longer explanations of their concerns and mentioned more discrete and specific symptoms—so they were more likely to be homing in on the real problem. As an added bonus, the doctors who asked the more general questions also received higher evaluation scores from patients.

When you ask the Lazy Question or another, more general opening question, the science tells us, you're not only more effective, but you're also more respected.

# Question
# Masterclass
# Part 6

# Actually **Listen** to the Answer

**Y**ou ask one of the Seven Essential Questions.

And then you move into Black-Belt Active Listening mode.

Nodding your head like a well-sprung bobblehead doll.

Making small grunting noises of encouragement.

Maintaining eye contact at all costs.

Yet rattling around in your head is a riot of distraction. Perhaps you're worrying about what question you should ask next. Perhaps you're thinking about how to get this whole conversation wrapped up as fast as possible. Perhaps you're wondering whether it's your turn to cook tonight, and whether you have enough garlic in the cupboard or if perhaps you should pick some up on the way home.

In any case, the wheel is spinning but the hamster is dead.*

One of the most compelling things you can do after asking a question is to *genuinely listen to the answer*. Stay curious, my friend.

---

* No one seems to know where this phrase comes from. But whoever invented it, I salute you.

The wheel is spinning but the hamster is **dead**.

## Here's Your New Habit

WHEN THIS HAPPENS...

After I've asked a question...

INSTEAD OF...

Going through the motions of looking like I'm actively listening...

I WILL...

Actually listen. And when I get distracted (which I will), I'll come back and start listening again.

1   The Kickstart Question
What's on your mind?

2   The AWE Question
And what else?

3   The Focus Question
What's the real challenge here for you?

4   The Foundation Question
What do you want?

5   The Lazy Question
How can I help?

**6   The Strategic Question**

7   The Learning Question

# 6: The Strategic Question

In which you get to the heart of overwhelm and **discover the question at the heart of every good strategy.**

## More Impact. More Meaning.

. . . . . . . . . . . . . . . . . . . . . . . . . . . . . . . .

You know how there's some work that you do that you absolutely love? It's the work that absorbs you and excites you. It's not just that the work is making a difference and having an impact; it's that the work means something to you. Frankly, this is the work that, when you signed up for this job, you hoped you'd be doing.

And then there's all that *other* work you've got to get through.

At Box of Crayons, we make the distinction between Good Work (the everyday, get-it-done, this-is-my-job-description type of work) and Great Work (the work with both more meaning and more impact), all with the goal of helping organizations and their people do less Good Work and more Great Work.

You can probably imagine how things might shift if you and your team were all doing, say, 10 percent more Great Work. But quite frankly, who has the time? In fact, if the chapter about the Lazy Question ("How can I help?") makes you a little uneasy, you might be fearing that someone will actually give you an answer. You're already behind on emails, meetings, deliverables, exercise, reading and family time. You're at full capacity. How could you possibly say Yes to anything more?

## Let's Ban "It's a Good Busy"

At the same time, perversely, in these hurly-burly days of end-less connectivity, lean organizations and globalization, it's *de rigueur* to humblebrag about being overcommitted and overwhelmed.

"How are you doing?" they ask.

"Busy," you reply. "But a *good* busy."

We're slowly waking up to the fact that being busy is no measure of success. George Bernard Shaw was on to something years ago when one of his maxims for revolutionaries stated, "The reasonable man adapts himself to the world: the unreasonable one persists in trying to adapt the world to himself. Therefore all progress depends on the unreasonable man." *4-Hour Workweek* author Tim Ferriss drove the point home recently when he said, "Being busy is a form of laziness—lazy thinking and indiscriminate action." (And that's *not* the good type of laziness I was promoting in the previous chapter.)

## Let's Also Ban "Work Smarter, Not Harder"

People have lots of snappy advice for you. "Work smarter, not harder." "Be more strategic." These maxims tend to be TBU: True But Useless sound bites that sound good but are impossible to act upon. In fact, "strategic" has become an overused qualifier, something we add to anything that we want to sound more important, more useful, more thoughtful, more ... good. This isn't just a meeting. It's a strategic meeting. A strategic report. A strategic lunch date. A strategic purchase of that fantastic pair of Jeffery West shoes I can't really afford but have been admiring for a while.

It can all leave employees supremely indifferent to the idea of strategy. When you combine the overuse of the term with the fact that anything to do with strategy is often seen as being "*their* work"—when "they" are anyone two or three levels higher than the employees—well, you're likely to encounter a nasty but predictable case of the SPOTS: Strategic Plans on Top Shelf.

But strategy isn't a thick PowerPoint document gathering dust somewhere. It's far more fundamental and common than that. Of the many definitions of "strategy" that I've seen, I think I like Michael Porter's best, when he said, "The essence of strategy is choosing what not to do."

## The Strategic Question: If You're Saying Yes to This, What Are You Saying No To?

This question is more complex than it sounds, which accounts for its potential. To begin with, you're asking people to be clear and committed to their Yes. Too often, we kinda sorta half-heartedly agree to something, or more likely, there's a complete misunderstanding in the room as to what's been agreed to. (Have you ever heard or uttered the phrase, "I never said I was going to do that!"? Me too.) So to ask, "Let's be clear: What exactly are you saying Yes to?" brings the commitment out of the shadows. If you then ask, "What could being fully committed to this idea look like?" it brings things into even sharper, bolder focus.

But a Yes is nothing without the No that gives it boundaries and form. And in fact, you're uncovering two types of No answers here—the No of omission and the No of commission. The first type of No applies to the options that are automatically eliminated by your saying Yes. If you say Yes to this meeting, you're saying No to something else that's happening at the same time as the meeting. Understanding this kind of No helps you understand the implications of the decision.

The second type of No you're uncovering—which will likely take the conversation another level deeper—is what you now *need* to say to make the Yes happen. It's all too easy to shove another Yes into the bag of our overcommitted lives, hoping that in a Harry Potter magical sort of way it will somehow all be accommodated. This second type of No puts the spotlight on how to create the space and focus, energy and resources that you'll need to truly do that Yes.

You can use the 3P model you read about in the Kickstart Question chapter to make sure you cover all the bases.

A **Yes**
is nothing
without
the **No**
that gives it
boundaries
and form.

### Projects

What projects do you need to abandon or postpone?
What meetings will you no longer attend?
What resources do you need to divert to the Yes?

### People

What expectations do you need to manage?
From what Drama Triangle dynamics will you extract yourself?
What relationships will you let wither?

### Patterns

What habits do you need to break?
What old stories or dated ambitions do you need to update?
What beliefs about yourself do you need to let go of?

## When Should You Say No?
## (And When Should You Say Yes?)

I asked my LinkedIn community what they thought were good reasons and bad reasons to say either Yes or No.

Here are some of the answers they gave me.

| BAD REASONS TO SAY... | GOOD REASONS TO SAY... |
|---|---|
| **YES** I'll do anything to have you get off the phone or leave the office.<br><br>I know that I'm not actually going to do it.<br><br>I think this will make people really like me.<br><br>Habit. | I was curious about the request and asked questions, and the person gave me good answers.<br><br>I'm clear on what I'm going to stop doing so I can start doing this.<br><br>It's Great Work for me—work that will have an impact and that means something.<br><br>My boss has made it clear that it's not negotiable. |
| **NO** I don't like the person. (Unless I really don't like the person.)<br><br>I'm comfortable and I don't want things to change.<br><br>Attack is the best form of defence.<br><br>Habit. | I was curious about the request and asked questions, and the person gave me good answers, so now I know it's not a fit.<br><br>I've thought about what my core priorities are, and I'm willing to hold the line.<br><br>I'm trying to build a reputation as someone who's strategic and thoughtful. |

## How to Say No When You Can't Say No (Part 1)

For most of us, there are two groups of people to whom it is easiest to say No. Those closest to us—spouses and kids—and those distant from us—hello, evening telemarketers. It's much harder to say No to everyone else. Which, unfortunately, tends to be everyone we work with. That difficulty is exacerbated by most corporate cultures, where the default answer is "Yes" or, at the bare minimum, "Probably."

Hear an interview with BILL JENSEN at the Great Work Podcast.

Bill "Mr. Simplicity" Jensen taught me that the secret to saying No was to shift the focus and learn how to say Yes more slowly. What gets us into trouble is how quickly we commit, without fully understanding what we're getting ourselves into or even why we're being asked.

Saying Yes more slowly means being willing to stay curious before committing. Which means asking more questions:

* Why are you asking me?

* Whom else have you asked?

* When you say this is urgent, what do you mean?

* According to what standard does this need to be completed? By when?

* If I couldn't do all of this, but could do just a part, what part would you have me do?

* What do you want me to take off my plate so I can do this?

Being willing to stay curious like this will likely provoke one of four types of responses, three of which might be helpful.

The first response, and the one that's not useful, is that the person tells you to stop with the annoying questions and just get on with the task. Depending on the person, the culture and the

# Saying Yes more slowly means being willing to **stay curious before committing**.

urgency of the task, sometimes it's clear that you're expected to do what you're told.

The second response is that he has good answers to all your questions. That's a win for you because it means that the request was thoughtful, and he's not asking you just because you have a pulse and yours was the first email address that started to populate the "To" address line.

Third, he doesn't have the answers but might be willing to find them for you. That's good. That buys you time, at a minimum, and it's quite possible that he'll never get back to you.

And finally, he may just say this: "You're too much like hard work. I'm going to find someone who says Yes more quickly than you do."

In a 2002 *Harvard Business Review* article, "Beware the Busy Manager," Heike Bruch and Sumantra Ghoshal suggested that only 10 percent of managers had the right focus and energy to work on the stuff that matters. To be frank, 10 percent sounds high to me. But most likely you can think of someone in your organization who seems to be able to "hold the line" and stop that aggregation of small tasks and additional responsibilities that, for the rest of us, eventually consume our lives. That person might not be the best-liked person in the organization—the need to be liked drives that Drama-Triangle Rescuer response of "Yes, I'll do that"—but she's likely to be successful, senior and respected.

And that's because she knows how to say Yes more slowly than you do.

## How to Say No When You Can't Say No (Part 2)

It's awkward saying No to something, because actually you're saying No to someone. And now people are involved, so we're into the messy awkwardness of dashing hopes, stomping on toes and having people think that you've let them down.

One secret from the world of facilitation, which we saw in a different context in the discussion about Coaching the Ghost, is to create a "third point"—an object that you can identify as the thing you're saying No to, which isn't the person. For instance, if you write down someone's request on a bit of paper or a flip chart, you can then point to it and say, "I'm afraid I have to say No to this," which is a little better than "I'm afraid I have to say No to you."

Say Yes to the person, but say No to the task.

## The Other Five Strategic Questions

Hear an interview with ROGER MARTIN at the Great Work Podcast.

There are an awful lot of books on strategy, and most of them you can skip. If you were to go and grab just one book on the topic, here's the one I'd recommend: Roger Martin and A.G. Lafley's *Playing to Win*. Lafley was Procter & Gamble's CEO during a period of great success (and was so good he came back for a second stint), and Martin—former dean of the University of Toronto's Rotman School of Management and a successful author—was his trusted advisor. They break strategy down into just five core questions that need to be answered—five questions that scale down to the individual and the team, and scale up to a complex, global, multibillion-dollar organization.

These questions are not linear. Answering one will influence the answer to the one that follows and likely to the one that preceded it. It is the process of working back and forth between them, creating alignment between your answers, that is

TO BE ON A QUEST IS NOTHING MORE OR LESS THAN TO **BECOME AN ASKER OF QUESTIONS.**

Sam Keen

the strength of this process. It was Eisenhower who said, "Plans are useless, but planning is indispensable," and while that's a little black and white, it's also true that the result of these questions is that they force great planning. Here are the five questions:

- **What is our winning aspiration?** Framing the choice as "winning" rules out mediocrity as an option. If you want to win, you need to know what game you're playing and with (and against) whom. What impact do you want to have in and on the world?

- **Where will we play?** "Boiling the ocean" is rarely successful. Choosing a sector, geography, product, channel and customer allows you to focus your resources.

- **How will we win?** What's the defendable difference that will open up the gap between you and the others?

- **What capabilities must be in place?** Not just what do you need to do, but how will it become and stay a strength?

- **What management systems are required?** It's easy enough to measure stuff. It's much harder to figure out what you want to measure that actually matters.

The question behind the questions is our Strategic Question: What will you say No to if you're truly saying Yes to this? Martin and Lafley put it like this: "Do remember that strategy is about winning choices. It is the coordinated and integrated set of five very specific choices. As you define your strategy, choose what you will do and what you will not do." Meg Whitman, CEO of HP (and such a fan of *Playing to Win* that she's made every manager read it) puts it thus: the process "forces the tough trade-offs."

## Build Your New Habit Here

· · · · · · · · · · · · · · · · · · · · · · · · · ·

**WHEN THIS HAPPENS...**

*Write out the moment, the person and perhaps the feelings that are your trigger.*

...............................................................................

...............................................................................

...............................................................................

...............................................................................

...............................................................................

The trigger here is when you see that someone's about to move from overwhelmed to really overwhelmed by adding more to their list. Or when they're wimping out by not making a choice but fudging things by saying Yes to everything. Or when the pace of work is just getting to be too much and you can see scope creep happening for people and their projects. In short, whenever someone's making a decision to commit to something new.

INSTEAD OF...

*Write out the old habit you want to stop doing. Be specific. For this question, it could have something to do with taming your Advice Monster.*

...............................................................................

...............................................................................

...............................................................................

...............................................................................

...............................................................................

The "instead of..." is when you hope that you and your team can defy the laws of physics and just keep adding more stuff to your capacity. So it's when you notice yourself in Rescuer mode (where you say Yes to everything to keep them happy) or Victim mode (when you feel you have no choice but to say Yes), and you want to pull out of that.

I WILL...

*Describe your new habit.*

...............................................................................

...............................................................................

...............................................................................

........................................................................

........................................................................

........................................................................

........................................................................

Stop the rush to action and towards the Cliffs of Overwhelm, and ask, "What will you say No to, to make this Yes rock-solid and real?"

## WATCH IT WORK

Watch the short videos at **TheCoachingHabit.com/videos** to deepen your learning and help turn insight into action.

### RAPID-FIRE STRATEGIC THINKING PLANNING & DOING

If you're wanting to up your strategic game, then the Strategic Question is a great place to start. If you want more than what's presented in this video, we share a one-page strategic planning tool that will give your plans a new focus and rigour.

**HOW TO SAY NO (WHEN YOU CAN'T SAY NO)** Saying No is tricky, particularly if you work in an organizational culture where Yes is the expected answer. In this video, you'll find strategies to build up your No muscle.

## FROM THE BOX OF CRAYONS LAB

Daniel Kahneman won the Nobel prize in economics in 2002 for his work on the psychology of judgment and decision-making, and the field more generally known as behavioural economics. He's best known for his book *Thinking, Fast and Slow,* which explains that we have two decision-making processes: a fast, instinctual "gut-feeling" one, and a slower, more rational one. The fast-thinking approach is very good and accurate—except when it isn't, and then our various cognitive biases make for very poor decision-making indeed. The Strategy Question can help us avoid at least two of these biases.

The first bias is the *planning fallacy*, which can be summed up as saying that we're lousy at figuring out how much time something will take us to complete. It's a combination of overestimating our abilities and, to add insult to injury, underestimating the degree to which we are overestimating. We think we can do more than we can; the Strategy Question helps us be more realistic about what's actually possible.

The second bias, known as *prospect theory*, tells us that loss and gain are not measured equally. Losing $100, say, feels worse than gaining $100 feels good. One result of the bias is that once we've got something, not only do we not want to let it go, but we also tend to overvalue its worth. Asking the Strategy Question shines a light on what we're holding on to, so we might better weigh up what's worth keeping and what might need to be set free.

# Question
# Masterclass
# Part 7

# **Acknow-ledge** the Answers You Get

Carly Rae Jepsen's 2012 summertime hit "Call Me Maybe" was more than a little popular. The video (with its great twist at the end) has north of 700 million views on YouTube. The song is also one of the latest examples of a very old form of music, call and response. Carly Rae sings ("Hey, I just met you") and the music responds (cue violins). Carly Rae sings again ("And this is crazy"), and again the music replies. You can trace this pattern back through classics like Muddy Waters' "Mannish Boy" to the deep roots of folk music and blues.

You're now fully aware of the Advice Monster, and you're staying focused on the questions rather than rushing to offer advice and suggestions. Bravo. Now bring in the structure of the call and response. Remember to *acknowledge the person's answers* before you leap to the next "And what else?"

You don't need to say much. This isn't about judging people; it's about encouraging them and letting them know that you listened and heard what they said.

This isn't about judging people; **it's about encouraging them.**

Some of my favourite replies are:

**FANTASTIC.**          **I LIKE IT.**                    **GOOD ONE.**

**NICE.**               **YES, THAT'S GOOD.**            **MMM-HMMM.**

I bet you've got some of your own, too. What would you add to this list?

## Here's Your New Habit

. . . . . . . . . . . . . . . . . . . . . . . .

WHEN THIS HAPPENS...

The person gives an answer to a question I've asked...

INSTEAD OF...

Rushing on to the next question...

I WILL...

Acknowledge the reply by saying, "Yes, that's good."

1 The Kickstart Question

What's on your mind?

2 The AWE Question

And what else?

3 The Focus Question

What's the real challenge here for you?

4 The Foundation Question

What do you want?

5 The Lazy Question

How can I help?

6 The Strategic Question

If you're saying Yes to this, what are you saying No to?

**7 The Learning Question**

# 7: The Learning Question

In which you discover how to finish any conversation in a way that will make you **look like a genius**.

## How People Learn

s a manager and a leader, you want people to get stuff done. But you want more than that. You want them to learn so that they become more competent, more self-sufficient and more successful. Conveniently, they want that as well.

But helping people learn is difficult. Sometimes it feels like even though you've hit them across the head repeatedly with an obvious concept (or a shovel perhaps), somehow the point you've been trying to make hasn't stuck. Here's why:

People don't really learn when you tell them something.

They don't even really learn when they do something.

They start learning, start creating new neural pathways, only when they have a chance to recall and reflect on what just happened.

## The Learning Question:
## "What Was Most Useful for You?"
. . . . . . . . . . . . . . . . . . . . . . . . . . . . . . . . . . .

Academic Chris Argyris coined the term for this "double-loop learning" more than forty years ago. If the first loop is trying to fix a problem, the second loop is creating a learning moment about the issue at hand. It's in the second loop where people pull back and find the insight. New connections get made. Aha moments happen.

Your job as a manager and a leader is to help create the space for people to have those learning moments. And to do that, you need a question that drives this double-loop learning. That question is, "What was most useful for you?"

## The Neuroscience of Learning
. . . . . . . . . . . . . . . . . . . . . . . . . . . . . . . . .

If you spend any time in the world of learning and development, you know that one of the deepest frustrations is the low retention rate of knowledge. Way too often, most people forget almost everything pretty much the moment they walk out of the corporate classroom. A week later, and even the most critical wisdom and insights so diligently presented are but faint and distant echoes. You've probably experienced exactly this on the other side of the classroom desk, where you've given up a day or two for a class, and the material has washed through you and over you, leaving very little behind.

Your job
is to **create
the space**
for those
learning
moments.

But we know how to make the learning experience more successful, thanks to insights from neuroscience and psychology. Josh Davis and colleagues from the NeuroLeadership Institute have created the AGES model to explain the four main neurological drivers of longer-term memory. "AGES" stands for Attention, Generation, Emotion and Spacing. What's useful here for us is the G: Generation. This is "the act of creating (and sharing) your own connections to new and presented ideas... When we take time and effort to generate knowledge and find an answer rather than just reading it, our memory retention is increased."

This is why, in a nutshell, advice is overrated. I can tell you something, and it's got a limited chance of making its way into your brain's hippocampus, the region that encodes memory. If I can ask you a question and you generate the answer yourself, the odds increase substantially.

## "To Learn, Retrieve"

A related insight comes from the world of psychology and, in particular, the excellent book *Make It Stick: The Science of Successful Learning* by Peter Brown, Henry Roediger and Mark McDaniel. The authors are distinguished psychology professors, and together they've created a useful summary of the best strategies and tactics we have to help people learn. The first major tactic they share is harnessing the impact of information retrieval. They put it beautifully: "What's essential is to interrupt the process of forgetting." That forgetting starts happening immediately, so even by asking the question at the end of a conversation, you've created the first interruption in that slide towards "I've never heard that before!"

And if you want to up the ante, you can find a way for this question to pop up in places other than the end of a conversation. The authors say, "Reflection is a form of practice"; create these moments and you find a place for Dan Coyle's Deep Practice. One option is to ask the question at the start of the team meeting or the regularly scheduled one-on-one. "What have you learned since we last met?" One of the disciplines I (mostly) follow at the end of my day is using an app called iDoneThis, and rather than just writing out what I did, I write down a sentence or two about what I learned and what I'm most proud of.

## Why "What Was Most Useful for You?" Tops the List

There are a number of questions you could ask to help drive this generative and retrieval process to embed the learning. "What did you learn?" "What was the key insight?" "What do you want to remember?" and "What's important to capture?" are some of the more obvious ways to help people do that, and they're all good questions.

But "What was most useful for you?" is like a superfood—kale perhaps—compared with the mere iceberg-lettuce goodness of the other questions. "What was most useful?" helps hits the spot in at least six ways.

### It Assumes the Conversation Was Useful

Winston Churchill said that people "occasionally stumble over the truth, but most of them pick themselves up and hurry off as if nothing ever happened." That's equally true about the conversations you're having with those around you. There's wisdom to be found, but only if you hang around for a moment to take a look. The Learning Question immediately frames what just happened as something that was useful and creates a moment in which to figure out what it was.

### It Asks People to Identify the Big Thing That Was Most Useful

Less, rather than more, is often better when you're giving feedback. If you list twelve things that could be improved, everyone moves into overwhelm mode. More effective is finding the OBT—the One Big Thing—that's worth remembering.

This question will typically have the person focus on the one or two key takeaways from the conversation.

# WE LIVE IN THE WORLD **OUR QUESTIONS CREATE.**

David Cooperrider

### It Makes It Personal

Adding "for you" to the question takes it from the abstract to the personal, from the objective to the subjective. Now you're helping people create new neural pathways.

And of course, people are telling themselves what was useful, rather than your telling them what you think should be most useful. The former will always sound like better advice.

### It Gives You Feedback

Listen to the answer you get, because it's useful not just for the coachee but for you as well. It will give you guidance on what to do more of next time, and it will reassure you (if you need it) that you're being useful even when you're not giving advice but are asking questions instead.

### It's Learning, Not Judgment

You'll notice that you're not asking, "Was this useful?" That question sets up a Yes/No answer, and it doesn't actually prompt insight; it just elicits judgment. "What was most useful?" forces people to extract the value from the conversation.

### It Reminds People How Useful You Are to Them

Come the annual performance appraisal, and an employee is staring at the questionnaire, with the cursor hovering over the upward-feedback part of it. "Is my manager useful?" the question asks. And thinking back over the last year, he's struck by the fact that every single conversation with you has proven to be useful. Top marks.

## The Coaching Bookends: How to Start Fast & Finish Strong

With this question, you now complete the pair of questions known as the Coaching Bookends.

You start with the Kickstart Question: What's on your mind?

That takes you quickly into a conversation that matters, rather than meandering through small talk or spinning your wheels on data that's more distracting than it is useful.

As you look to complete your conversation, before everyone rushes for the door, you ask the Learning Question: What was most useful for you about this conversation?

Answering that question extracts what was useful, shares the wisdom and embeds the learning. If you want to enrich the conversation even further—and build a stronger relationship, too—tell people what you found to be most useful about the exchange. That equal exchange of information strengthens the social contract.

## Build Your New Habit Here

. . . . . . . . . . . . . . . . . . . . . . . . . . .

WHEN THIS HAPPENS...

*Write out the moment, the person and perhaps the feelings that are your trigger.*

................................................................................

................................................................................

................................................................................

................................................................................

................................................................................

This question is the second part of the Coaching Bookends, so the trigger moment is at the end of an exchange—in person or virtually. With a team member. A colleague. Your boss. At a team meeting. After giving a speech. When talking to a customer, prospect or client. If you're thinking to yourself, "Good, we're done!" then that's the time.

INSTEAD OF...

*Write out the old habit you want to stop doing. Be specific.*

................................................................................

................................................................................

................................................................................

..............................................................................

..............................................................................

It's in Shakespeare's *The Winter's Tale* where the most famous stage direction of all time resides: "Exit, pursued by a bear." That's how most conversations seem to end as well. Instead of asking the Learning Question, you wrap up, you tell people how wonderful they are, you check the action list or you worry about your next meeting because now you're late because this meeting ran over. The "instead of…" is any action that fails to capture the aha moment and extract the value.

I WILL...

*Describe your new habit.*

..............................................................................

..............................................................................

..............................................................................

..............................................................................

..............................................................................

You know it. "So, what was most useful here for you?" Or "What did you find most valuable about this chat?" Or "What worked best here?" Or some variation that asks people to artic-ulate the value and the learning.

**WATCH IT WORK**
Watch the short videos at TheCoachingHabit.com/videos to
deepen your learning and help turn insight into action.
**MAKE IT STICKY**  This video sets out strategies to make any
interaction more useful by helping the participants remember
the good stuff.

*   *   *

## FROM THE BOX OF CRAYONS LAB

I've shared in this chapter some of the science on how to
improve knowledge retrieval. So I asked our researcher, Lindsay, to find me something new and interesting to say about why
the Learning Question works as well as it does. She took me to
an unexpected place. Colonoscopies.

This next bit of information comes from more research by
Daniel Kahneman, this time on the *peak-end rule*. In short, how
we're evaluating an experience is disproportionately influenced
by the peak (or the trough) of the experience and by the ending
moments. Finish on a high note and you make everything that
went before it look better.

People have tested this theory in a number of ways, the most visceral being via colonoscopy. In one study, some patients received traditional colonoscopies, while others received modified procedures. Patients whose colonoscopies were extended by approximately one minute but who experienced less pain in the final moments report remembering 10 percent less pain overall and rank the procedure as less unpleasant compared with a list of other aversive experiences. These patients were also 10 percent more likely to return for a follow-up procedure.

"What was most useful here for you?" is a strong and positive way to finish a conversation. Not only do you help people to see and then embed the learning from the conversation, but by your finishing on a "this *was* useful" note, people are going to remember the experience more favourably than they otherwise might.

**1** The Kickstart Question

What's on your mind?

**2** The AWE Question

And what else?

**3** The Focus Question

What's the real challenge here for you?

**4** The Foundation Question

What do you want?

**5** The Lazy Question

How can I help?

**6** The Strategic Question

If you're saying Yes to this, what are you saying No to?

**7** The Learning Question

What was most useful for you?

# Question
# Masterclass
# Part 8

# Use Every Channel to **Ask a Question**

**W**e're at the end of the book, so I know that you've already got what it's about. You're going to change the way you have conversations with the people you manage, influence and engage with. You'll stay curious, tamp down the Advice Monster and help people quickly figure out their own paths, all while sharing your own advice and wisdom in the right dosage and at the right time.

And yet—a hefty and ever-increasing amount of our lives is spent staring at the screen, tap-tap-tapping away on keyboards as we exchange emails and IMs and texts and Slack messages and tweets and Facebook updates and [insert the names of the other 329 electronic channels you currently use one way or another].

And these Seven Essential Questions work just as well for those communication channels as they do face-to-face.

What that means could be radical for you. When you get the long rambling email, you'll be prepared. Whereas in the past you have sighed, metaphorically rolled up your sleeves and started to type out your long, advice-rich reply, now you can use one or more of these questions to focus faster and to spend less time in your inbox.

# Questions work just as well **typed** as they do spoken.

## Here's Your New Habit
. . . . . . . . . . . . . . . . . . . . . . . . .

WHEN THIS HAPPENS...

When I get an email that triggers the Advice Monster...

INSTEAD OF...

Writing out a long, thorough answer full of possible solutions, approaches and ideas, or even a short, terse answer with a single command...

I WILL...

Decide which one of the seven questions would be most appropriate, and ask that question by email. It could sound like:

"Wow, there's a lot going on here. What's the real challenge here for you, do you think?"

"I've scanned your email. In a sentence or two, what do you want?"

"Before I jump into a longer reply, let me ask you: What's the real challenge here for you?"

# Conclusion

## Survivorman. Not.

S till at university in Australia, I hadn't yet fully accepted my urban destiny.

I know now that I'm a city boy. I have the soft hands of a typist and not a single Do It Yourself or Survivor gene in my DNA.

But back then, I thought that perhaps I could still evolve into that Jason Bourne–esque man, the type who had 1 percent body fat and could survive in the outdoors for three weeks using nothing but three twigs and a handful of leaves.

In that spirit, I planned a solo three-day trek. I'd been bush-walking—that's Australian for "hiking"—before, so I wasn't totally ignorant of what I was proposing. And ten years earlier I'd got my knot-tying badge from the Boy Scouts. How hard could this be?

## Heavy

The scale said forty pounds, but in truth my backpack felt considerably heavier than that. I did know that approximately 90 percent of this weight was the first-aid kit. I was a little nervous about getting injured, so I was carrying remedies for all sorts of medical challenges, from snake bite to lightning strike.

But after a three-hour drive from home, I arrived at the start of the circuit I was going to walk and I was feeling good. The weather was fine and promised to hold. There were a few other cars in the car park, so I wouldn't be totally alone. And having done my research, I knew that this wasn't a difficult trek. It was just three days of doing it by myself.

The path started off clear and broad, but quickly it narrowed. After twenty minutes it had all but vanished. Indeed, I could figure out the way forward only by keeping a keen eye out for the knee-high grass that, in irregular intervals, some fellow traveller had tied knots in to mark the way. And then the knotted grass stopped as well.

Honestly, I was confused. The map seemed to indicate that the path was a big, obvious trail working its way up the mountain, and clearly the map was wrong. My path hadn't climbed up at all but had stayed pretty level, and it wasn't so much a path as it was a barely noticeable trail and ... ah. Hmmm.

I was lost.

## Forward or Back?

There were two ways forward from here. Well, one way wasn't forward at all. It would have involved trying to retreat along the path I'd come on. Obviously, as a man, I found this to be an unacceptable option.

The remaining route—bold, courageous and direct, a little like me—involved pointing myself directly up the side of the mountain. If I did that, it was inevitable that I'd cross the path and be back on track once more.

I don't have much memory of that climb. Just flashbacks. Balancing perilously on top of the moss-covered boulders of the waterfall. Trying to get through the impenetrable ti tree bushes by crawling on my belly and pushing the pack in front of me. Retreating from the impenetrable ti tree bushes on my belly and dragging the pack back with me. The creeping sense of foreboding and panic and aloneness.

Eventually I found the path. It was as wide and as obvious as the map had indicated. I, on the other hand, was scratched, bruised and exhausted. It had been just over seven hours since I'd left the car. I was broken. I decided to set up my tent for the night. Sure, I was making camp a little early, but I needed to recover and regroup.

With my cup of tea brewing over my campfire, I spied a fellow hiker coming towards me from the direction of the car park. He looked fresh. I hailed him. Not really wanting to talk about my experience of the day, I turned the conversation immediately to how the walk had been going for him so far.

It was hard to really say, he told me. He'd been walking for only fifteen minutes.

## What Has This Story Got to Do with the Coaching Habit?

I've been a manager and I've been managed. I've coached managers and I've trained managers to be more coach-like. In my experience, too many conversations between managers and those they're managing feel much too much like my ill-fated hike through the Budawang National Park:

* Too much baggage

* Too much certainty, thinking you know the destination and the path to get there

* Wandering off the path too quickly

* Working way too hard to get back on the path

* And being exhausted at the end, having got a lot less far down the track than you'd hoped you would

If that description feels true to you, then you'll be well served to build a coaching habit of your own. The questions here are the ones that I've found to have the most impact, and I do believe that if you can make just these Seven Essential Questions part of your management repertoire and everyday conversations, you'll work less hard and have more impact, and your people, your boss, your career and your life outside work will thank you for it.

But the real secret sauce here is building a habit of curiosity. The change of behaviour that's going to serve you most powerfully is simply this: a little less advice, a little more curiosity. Find your own questions, find your own voice. And above all, build your own coaching habit.

# A Treasure Trove

## of Additional Awesomeness

## Our "My One Best Question" Video Series

You know my favourite seven questions. But there are other great questions out there and other people who champion them.

We've been asking business leaders, executive coaches, brilliant authors and provocative thought leaders to share their one best question with us by video, as part of our "My One Best Question" project.

Contributors include best-selling authors and thought leaders such as Bev Kaye, Pam Slim, Michael Port, Jim Kouzes, Les McKeown, Lisa Bodell, Warren Berger and Teresa Amabile, as well as senior executives from such organizations as UBS, TELUS, Toys"R"Us, BBDO, Adobe, IHG and T-Mobile.

You can see all the video episodes at:
http://www.boxofcrayons.biz/category/best-question/

## My "Top-Shelf" Management Books

If you're a fan of a well-mixed cocktail like I am—email me at cocktail@boxofcrayons.biz if you'd like an outstanding recipe for a lavender margarita—you'll appreciate that the top shelf of any bar is where they keep "the good stuff."

I read more than a hundred business books a year, and I have done this for years. I have limited bookshelf space, and that means that if I want to keep a book, I have to let another one go. It's ruthless, it's Darwinian, and it means I'm really opinionated about which books I think can best help you perform at your best, live a good life and do more Great Work: the work that has an impact, the work that has meaning and the work that makes a difference. Here's my "top shelf."

Hear interviews with **DAN PINK,** **CHARLES DUHIGG,** **DAN SIEGEL** and **SETH GODIN** at the Great Work Podcast.

You can see (and order) these books at The CoachingHabit.com/Bookshelf, as well as video reviews of some of my favourite books.

## Self-Management

If you can read just one book on motivation—yours and others:
Dan Pink, **Drive**

If you can read just one book on building new habits:
Charles Duhigg, **The Power of Habit**

If you can read just one book on harnessing neuroscience for personal change:
Dan Siegel, **Mindsight**

If you can read just one book on deep personal change:
Lisa Lahey and Bob Kegan, **Immunity to Change**

If you can read just one book on resilience:
Seth Godin, **The Dip**

## Organizational Change

If you can read just one book on how organizational change really works:
Chip and Dan Heath, **Switch**

**Hear interviews with FREDERIC LALOUX, DAN PONTEFRACT and JERRY STERNIN at the Great Work Podcast.**

If you can read just two books on understanding that change is a complex system:
Frederic Laloux, **Reinventing Organizations**
Dan Pontefract, **Flat Army**

If you can read just one book on using structure to change behaviours:
Atul Gawande, **The Checklist Manifesto**

If you can read just one book on how to amplify the good:
Richard Pascale, Jerry Sternin and Monique Sternin, **The Power of Positive Deviance**

If you can read just one book on increasing your impact within organizations:
Peter Block, **Flawless Consulting**

## Other Cool Stuff

If you can read just one book on being strategic:
Roger Martin and A.G. Lafley, **Playing to Win**

If you can read just one book on scaling up your impact:
Bob Sutton and Huggy Rao, **Scaling Up Excellence**

**Hear interviews with ROGER MARTIN, BOB SUTTON and WARREN BERGER at the Great Work Podcast.**

If you can read just one book on being more helpful:
Edgar Schein, **Helping**

If you can read just two books on the great questions:
Warren Berger, **A More Beautiful Question**
Dorothy Strachan, **Making Questions Work**

If you can read just one book on creating learning that sticks:
Peter Brown, Henry Roediger and Mark McDaniel, **Make It Stick**

If you can read just one book on why you should appreciate and marvel at every day, every moment:
Bill Bryson, **A Short History of Nearly Everything**

If you can read just one book that saves lives while increasing impact:
Michael Bungay Stanier, ed., **End Malaria**
(All money goes to Malaria No More; about $400,000 has been raised so far.)

IF THERE ARE NO STUPID QUESTIONS, THEN **WHAT KIND OF QUESTIONS DO STUPID PEOPLE ASK**? DO THEY GET SMART JUST IN TIME TO ASK QUESTIONS?

Scott Adams

## From the Box of Crayons Lab: Our Sources

If you'd like to dig deeper into the science behind the questions, here are Lindsay's sources for her research:

### "What's On Your Mind?" Research

Weaver, S.M., and C.M. Arrington. "What's on Your Mind: The Influence of the Contents of Working Memory on Choice." *Quarterly Journal of Experimental Psychology* 63, 4 (2010): 726–37.

### "And What Else?" Research

Evans, Angela D., and Kang Lee. "Emergence of Lying in Very Young Children." *Developmental Psychology* 49, 10 (2013): 1958–63.

Gilson, Cindy M., C.A. Little, A.N. Ruegg, and M. Bruce-Davis. "An Investigation of Elementary Teachers' Use of Follow-Up Questions for Students at Different Reading Levels." *Journal of Advanced Academics* 25, 2 (2014): 101–28.

Lowe, M.L., and C.C. Crawford. "First Impression versus Second Thought in True-False Tests." *Journal of Educational Psychology* 20, 3 (1929): 192–95.

### "What's the Real Challenge for You Here?" Research

d'Ailly, H.H., J. Simpson, and G.E. MacKinnon. "Where Should 'You' Go in a Math Compare Problem?" *Journal of Educational Psychology* 89, 3 (1997): 562–67.

## "What Do You Want?" Research

Weatherall, A., and M. Gibson. "'I'm Going to Ask You a Very Strange Question': A Conversation Analytic Case Study of the Miracle Technique in Solution-Based Therapy." *Qualitative Research in Psychology* 12, 2 (2015): 162–81.

## "How Can I Help?" Research

Heritage, J., and J.D. Robinson. "The Structure of Patients' Presenting Concerns: Physicians' Opening Questions." *Health Communication* 19, 2 (2006): 89–102.

Robinson, J.D., and J. Heritage. "Physicians' Opening Questions and Patients' Satisfaction." *Patient Education and Counseling* 60, 3 (2006): 279–85.

## "What Are You Saying No To?" Research

Kahneman, D., and A. Tversky. "On the Psychology of Prediction." *Psychological Review* 80, 4 (1973): 237–51.

Kahneman, D., and A. Tversky. "Prospect Theory: An Analysis of Decision under Risk." In P.K. Moser, ed., *Rationality in Action: Contemporary Approaches*, 140–70. New York: Cambridge University Press, 1990.

## "What Was Most Useful for You?" Research

Redelmeier, Donald A., Joel Katz, and Daniel Kahneman. "Memories of Colonoscopy: A Randomized Trial." *Pain* 104 (2003): 187–94.

# Acknowledgments

Writing an acknowledgment page is fraught with anxiety. You suddenly realize: one, just how many people have helped you get over the finish line; and, two, how fallible your memory is. I know I'm going to forget someone who should not be forgotten. If you're that person, my apologies.

It's taken me more than four years to get this book written, and along the way I wrote three versions of it that weren't very good. At all. So the usefulness and elegance of this is due to the encouragement and enthusiasm and talents of a rather large group of people.

Supportive readers of various sucky versions of the book include Jill Murphy, Kate Lye, Jen Louden, Pam Slim, Michael Leckie, Karen Wright, Eric Klein, Molly Gordon, Mark Silver, Venita Indewey and Gus Stanier, all of whom managed to encourage me to go on while steering me away from mediocrity. Suzie Bolotin and Bruce Tracy at Workman said no to earlier versions, which proved to be astute. Lindsay Miller and Elizabeth Woodworth helped me ground my work with insightful research.

I've had a fantastic editorial and design team. Catherine Oliver of Oliver Editorial Services stopped me using so many ellipses...And Capital Letters...and much more. She's shaped this manuscript through three rounds of editing, from big-picture changes to fine-tuning the minutiae (and thank you Seth for the connection). Judy Phillips brought an eagle eye to the proofreading. Jesse Finkelstein and Megan Jones of Page Two, my publishing consultants, have helped us navigate the landscape of self-publication as savvy professionals rather than stumbling amateurs. And Peter Cocking has designed a book that has elegance and style, a book I love for its look and feel, not just for its content. My co-conspirator Mark Bowden came up with the book's subtitle, which is perfect.

Box of Crayons has an extraordinary team of people who we feel lucky to have help us make our dint in the universe. Thank you to Charlotte Riley, Denise Aday, Ana Garza-Robillard, Peter Hatch, Sonia Gaballa, Sylvana La Selva, Ernest Oriente, Rona Birenbaum, Warren McCann, Frank Merran. A special "hat tip" to Robert Kabwe of Poplogik, who has helped shape the design of this book, and to Stan McGee, who helped plan and run the marketing of the book's launch.

Box of Crayons specializes in helping busy managers coach in ten minutes or less, and our programs are delivered by a wonderful group of master facilitators. Thanks to our current faculty, Lea Belair, Helene Bellerose, Jamie Broughton, Tina Dias, Jonathan Hill, Leanne Lewis and Susan Lynne. You can learn more about each of these lovely people at BoxOfCrayons.biz.

Someone once said behind every successful man is a surprised woman. Marcella Bungay Stanier, VP of Everything Else, and Marlene Eldemire, head of the ICU (Internal Crayons Unit), are the women in this case. Thank you both for your support and love and encouragement.

# About the Author

"**My name is Michael**. I can hop. Do you want to see me hop?" This was how the three-year-old Michael introduced himself to surprised strangers in supermarkets. Here's a slightly more polished version of that.

You can read about Michael's official accomplishments at **boxofcrayons.biz**. If you're interested in origin stories, Michael knocked himself unconscious as a labourer by hitting himself in the head with a shovel, received his first cheque as an author for a romantic story called "The Male Delivery" and mastered stage craft at law school when he appeared in a skit called *Synchronized Nude Male Modelling*. His real success in becoming a Rhodes Scholar and going to Oxford was meeting and marrying a Canadian who refuses to take him too seriously.

LinkedIn is the best place to connect directly with Michael. He's the only Bungay Stanier there, so he's easy to find.

# Bring The Coaching Habit into your organization

Since 2008 Box of Crayons has given more than 10,000 busy managers practical tools for everyday coaching. What if your managers and leaders could coach in 10 minutes or less?

## A foundation skill

Coaching can increase focus and capacity, reduce overwhelm and dependency, and drive engagement and impact. But even with the best of intentions, today's busy managers find themselves defaulting to an old-school management approach: tell them rather than ask them; solve it for them rather than help them figure it out.

Theory, models and exhortations to "do more coaching" just aren't going to cut it. We need to help managers and leaders change their behaviour so that coaching becomes a regular and useful part of their management repertoire.

## Give your managers The Coaching Habit

**The Coaching Habit** is an innovative and award-winning program that changes behaviour in three ways.

First, participants understand why they're so quick to jump in and be the advice giver and the problem solver—and the price everyone pays as a result. With this new understanding, it becomes easier to disarm the advice-giving "hair-trigger" so that managers can use their coaching skills when the occasion calls for it.

Second, we share a select range of practical next-day-ready coaching tools to increase focus, engagement and impact, and show how people can convert these new insights into new habits.

Finally, we establish an innovative 108-day follow-up process to the program to help embed the new tools, skills and behaviours and get it "in their bones."

**"I'm seeing application of the content, which you don't very often see in a business setting. And there's an increased level of self-awareness as well, so they can build on their own leadership ability and get better at it."**

**TODD GILCHREST**, SVP HR, Capital Power

## Learning that sticks

**The Coaching Habit** is highly interactive, practical and fun, and draws on the very latest psychological insights and neuroscience to help the learning stick.

Organizations such as TD Bank, UBS, EllisDon, Fidelity Investments, AstraZeneca, Lowe's and Nokia have made **The Coaching Habit** a key part of their organizational growth.

"I expect to see results immediately... and with this program I did. I know that the learning resonated and has stuck."

**MARIE CREA**, Director of Talent, Horizon Blue Cross Blue Shield

You can learn more at BoxOfCrayons.biz
or contact us directly at inquiry@BoxOfCrayons.